Time Bomb

HOW POPULATION AGING WILL TRANSFORM OUR WORLD AND WHY WE MUST ACT BEFORE IT'S TOO LATE

MARK ADLER

ISBN: 9781099955310 (paperback)

Without any major changes in entitlements, entitlements are going to rise. Why? Because the population is aging. There's no way to reverse that and the politics of it are awful.

Alan Greenspan
Chairman, Federal Reserve Bank of the United States,
1987-2006
CNBC - April 12, 2019

Dedicated to my wife and children.

Table of Contents

Every effort has been taken to ensure the accuracy of the
information contained within this publication.

Introduction

On a business trip to Washington, D.C., in early 2007, I stopped in to visit a friend who had recently been elected to the United States House of Representatives. For anyone who has been to a Representative's office on Capitol Hill knows that the Member's reception area is constantly filled with constituents, representatives of interest groups, or lobbyists all patiently awaiting their turn to meet with the Congressman. It was no different that time. While seated, I struck up a conversation with a very friendly elderly fellow sitting next to me.

When I told him I was from Toronto, well, his face lit up. He had just returned from a recent trip to the city. He went on glowingly about how much he loves the city. He especially liked how ethnocultural it was seeing people from all parts of the world. But, more importantly, Toronto held a very special place in his heart. The summer before, his granddaughter married a fellow from Canada and the two had their wedding ceremony just north of the city in an old church in Muskoka.

After the wedding, he said the couple moved to Ottawa where he was looking forward to visiting them once the weather warmed up a bit. I asked him what brought him to D.C. He told me he was there on behalf of a group of former United States Marines that were trying to get funding to help construct a recreation centre in the Congressman's district. The centre would be open to all but would be built in honour of all the military veterans, of which he included himself, who had served their country.

As we continued to chat, I began to wonder where he had done his service. He looked to be in his mid 70s, so I assumed he had served in the Korean War. A logical assumption given his very grandfatherly appearance. However, was I ever wrong. He was a veteran of the Vietnam War. Turns out he did three tours in Vietnam culminating in the Tet offensive in 1968. He was wounded in the leg in Saigon and was sent home.

As we continued to talk and get to know each other, I couldn't help but ask myself how this gray haired elderly looking fellow could possibly have served in Vietnam. Although just a child at the time of the Vietnam War, I remember the news reports so vividly. The American soldiers were all so young. Just kids. But then it occurred to me that those memories are from fifty years ago and I was no longer seven years old either. In the intervening half century we had all aged some. Then I remembered what a friend of mine, a few years my senior, had mentioned just about a week before I had this encounter in Washington ... *Why does everyone my age look so old?*

On the flight home that evening, I began to think about that encounter with my new friend and just how quickly the intervening years seem to go by. Then like the flash powder that would explode on the turn of the centuries photographer's tray, I began to think about growing up in the late 1960s and 1970s. Just how many young people there were everywhere. A total culture of youth. Then I began to wonder what became of all those young people. All those who Don McLean described in his song, American Pie, released in 1971, as *A generation lost in space*. Or, more commonly known as, the baby boom generation.

This is how I became interested in demographics and population aging. Sparked by a discussion with a Vietnam veteran during a visit to my friend's Congressional office in Washington, D.C

A mere chance chat that led me to what has become a passion. The world's shifting demographic structure and the implications it has on public policy, geopolitics, international affairs, trade policy, economics, finance and social policy. It has consumed my interest now for more than a decade.

Delving into every book, study and report I could get my hands on, I voraciously began to read everything on population aging. Naturally, it did not take long for me to see how our world's rapidly shifting demographics would have implications that are far and wide. These changes will impact every aspect of our society. What's more, policy makers will have some very difficult decisions to make over the forthcoming years.

As these decisions will involve the future character of our country, it will be of paramount importance to have as much input from the Canadian people as possible. The discussion of the issue that is contained within the following pages will hopefully spark that discussion. In addition, I have also established the National Organization on Aging and Longevity (NOAL). NOAL will provide thought leadership, strategic advice and innovative research to government and business on how to meet the challenges and opportunities posed by the world's rapidly shifting demographics.

That chance meeting in Washington is what ultimately led me to write this book. It is not intended to be an exhaustive study of shifting demographic structures, but rather more of a macro overview of the forthcoming challenges confronting governments and business within the framework of rapid population aging. Additional books that delve more thoroughly into specific topics will be published over time. But in the meantime, the hope of this work and that of the National Organization on Aging and Longevity is to begin a national discussion on the challenges and opportunities posed by our rapidly changing age distribution.

Canada has the dubious distinction of possessing one of the most rapidly aging populations in the world. This provides Canada with a unique opportunity to stand as a model country on how to transition to an aged society without compromising our cherished values of equality of opportunity, social justice and common destiny. It is our responsibility to ensure that future generations of Canadians inherit a country that is at least as just as the one we inherited ourselves.

1

What Is Population Aging?

Population aging, demographic aging and aging of the population, however anyone refers to it, all the means the same thing. The overall population is aging.

Wow! That's news? Of course everyone is aging. From the moment a newborn takes their first breath they are aging. So, what's the news here? Everyone alive is getting older. Thank you, Captain Obvious. Of course everyone is getting older. So just in case anyone was not aware by now, Spanish Explorer, Juan Ponce de Leon, did not find the Fountain of Youth when he stumbled upon Florida in 1513. So if everyone since Adam and Eve have aged over time, why should aging suddenly be of any great concern? If it's been occurring for almost six thousand years, surely it should come as no surprise to anyone that aging is still occurring. Surely everyone would be aware of it by now.

What is new, however, due to decades of sharply declining fertility rates and increasing longevity, the proportion and absolute number of older people have been surging. Defined as those members of a given population that have reached 65 years of age, this increase is occurring for the first time ever in human history.

Countries leading the way on this front are some of the largest in the world. Japan, with a median age of 47.3, followed by Germany at 47.1 and Italy 45.5, all G7 countries, combined account for a nominal GDP of 12.2% of global output. It is projected, that by 2050, the median age for each of these countries will be over 50 years. A fourth G7 country also on the aging fast track is Canada. Currently aging faster than any other country in the Western Hemisphere, the median age of Canada's population is 42.2 years.

Although populations have been aging in some instances for over a century, it has not been until recent decades that it has garnered much attention. Watch for this to change though. Population aging will be the biggest issue facing governments, business and every other aspect of society in the 21st century. Of particular note will be it's fiscal implications. Not only is population aging unprecedented, but it is permanent. As a result, borrowing to finance their way through the transition to an aged society is simply not an option. Fundamental change will be required.

The first signs of population aging occured in France in 1865. For much of France's history until the 19th century, it had the largest population in Europe and fourth in the world. However, by the beginning of the 19th century, the birth rate started to decline. In 1865, those persons 65 years and over in France constituted 7% of the population and exceeded those sixteen years of age and under by 10%. By current standards, this officially made France an aging society. It would take the country until 1980, to increase the size of it's population of 65 year olds and over to 14%.

France assumed the dubious distinction of having the world's first aging population. Before the French Revolution, which began in 1789, the country was governed by an absolute monarchy under a system referred to as the Ancien Regime. According to the regime's inheritance laws, anyone not belonging to the clergy or nobility were unable to will an estate to their next of kin upon their own demise. This had the effect of diminishing the fertility rate among those who were not members of the upper social castes. Although these laws were changed after the Revolution, the dye had been cast. France's population had begun to age.

A country's fertility rate can be influenced in a variety of ways. Although it may not have been the intent of French nobility to use the country's legislative levers to do so, the effect was just the same. The reason was more likely seen as an opportunity to usurp the property, possessions and any wealth that may have been accumulated by those in the lower castes. Low fertility turned out to be more collateral damage than policy intent. China, on the other hand, over a century later, through it's infamous *One-Child Policy*, certainly stands as a historic example of government profoundly, and with intent, use the policy tools of the state to influence the country's future demographic structure.

In addition to social engineering, there are other ways a population can age. The most common of these is when a country's population goes through a period of *demographic transition*. This is marked by a country's passage from an agrarian society marked by a high fertility and high mortality rate to an industrial society with low fertility and low mortality.

There are additional factors that can alter a country's demographic structure years and decades into the future. Some of these are: war, catastrophic natural disasters, level of gender equality, religious adherence, income, education, contraceptive use or a country's overall economic development and progress.

Although population aging is occurring around the world, it's pace and proportion vary from country to country. Currently, 17% of the world's population live in developed countries. However,

35% of those persons 65 years and over and more than 50% of all who are 85 years and over live in these same developed countries. Japan has the oldest population of any country. South Korea, Hong Kong and Taiwan are all aging very quickly and by 2050 are expected to be hot on the heels of Japan.

It took France 115 years for it's population of 65+ year olds to go from 7% of the population to 14%. By comparison, other countries are doing so in far less time. Singapore and South Korea, for instance, are making this move in only 19 years. For those countries aging at a quicker pace than others, they will be forced to confront the challenges posed by population aging sooner than those who are aging slower.

By 2050, only 33 countries in the world are projected to have a population 65 years and over that make up at least 7% of their total population. There are currently 115 countries in this category. A sharp decline in the global fertility rate has accelerated this trend. Since 1950, the global fertility rate has gone from five children per woman to 2.5 today.

Once a population of 65 year olds exceeds the number of those under sixteen years of age, it is declared to be an aged society. This is an important distinction to be made from a population that is aging. Although the former is a pre-condition for the latter, a population does not qualify as aged until the proportion of 65 year olds and over exceed the number of those persons under sixteen years of age. Even though a population can be declared aged, it can still, however, continue to age.

It is acknowledged in all quarters that population aging will fundamentally alter the way societies and economies function. For those countries aging faster, they will have a shorter period of time to prepare their infrastructure, healthcare systems and social institutions to accommodate an older population. The expected length of time a country's population ages is significant because it dictates the amount of time it has to adjust to the changing age structure.

As a population skews older, its society will develop different needs than it had previously. What's more, since this is the first time in human history that populations are aging, there is no precedent to draw on for best practices.

By understanding their own shifting demographics, governments can anticipate and plan for an aged society. In order to do so, however, societies will need to dispose of all ageist stereotypes and ageism. In other words, discrimination based on a person's age. Changing public infrastructure is difficult enough, but altering attitudes and mindsets is a far more challenging a task. Discarding negative notions of older people as a burden and replacing it with a belief that age should not stand as an impediment to full and active participation in society will be a much more difficult task.

Societies really need to rethink cultural expectations of what *old* really means. The definition of old is changing as life expectancy increases. Let's face it, someone's age is just the number of years they have been alive. Yet, in spite of increasing longevity, people are still defined by their age as it was perceived decades ago. So, someone in their mid 60s, is still considered old by many even though average life expectancy can be in the early to mid eighties in some countries.

In most countries, upon reaching 65 years of age, a person becomes what is referred to as a senior citizen. It is at this age that government programmes such as, old age security, prescription drug benefits and specific income tax applications become available. It is also the age many retailers and service outlets offer what they call *seniors' discounts* where a specific percentage off the price of an item for purchase.

But it's not all a basket of benefits. In many jurisdictions, if an employee is injured on the job, they are not eligible for workplace compensation. Many employer health plans use 65 as the cut off for ending health, dental and vision care insurance. Human rights codes do not tend to protect employee benefits for those who continue to work past 65. The assumption is that once a person turns 65 years of age they should rely on government social programmes and not costly private coverage provided by an employer.

International non-governmental organizations such as the World Health Organization, United Nations and the International Monetary Fund, also use 65 years and the embarkation point for old age. Statistical agencies and data collection offices of national governments also typically use 65 years to define the start of old age. While younger ages are segmented usually by decade, 65 years and over tend to serve as one single data set. The implication, of course being, that 65 years and over is just considered to be, old.

Like art, age appears to be in the eye of the beholder. Studies show, when asked *When does old age begin?*, the younger the respondent, the younger the age. So, millenials will say old age begins at 55. For Generation X, it's late 60s and for baby boomers old age does not begin until a person reaches their late 70s.

Perhaps the comparison below will shed some light. On the right, is of course the famous portrait of Whistler's Mother. Painted in 1871, Anna McNeill Whistler was 67 years of age when this painting of her was completed. Compare Anna Whistler to the photo of actor Jane Fonda at 80 years of age. In spite of being thirteen years her junior, Anna Whistler looks far older than Jane Fonda. For that matter, she also appears much older than most other women today of the same age.

Not only are people living longer, healthier and more active lives than they were mere decades ago, they are feeling and looking better than ever. Yet, society, culture, institutions and public policy continue to use 65 years as the benchmark for retirement and old age.

So, what is it about 65 years of age that is so sacrosanct that it makes governments and societies shudder at the mere thought of changing it? It's worthy to note that the age of 65, that is used almost universally, has a rather interesting history.

One would think that it's selection was made after careful study and copious research. Actuarial tables would have been analyzed by a team of some of the most notable economists, mathematicians and statistical experts at the time. After all this was done, the consensus reached was that the age of 65 years must be selected. One would think. However, nothing could be farther from the truth.

Rather, the selection of 65 as a retirement age was far more arbitrary. Proposed by Prussian Chancellor, Otto von Bismarck in 1881, to confront the growing popularity of Marxism within the working classes, he decided to institute a state pension for the country's older population. At the time, he selected the age of 70. The rationale was that average life expectancy was in the mid-fifties so few would actually live long enough for the government to have to pay out. All made perfect sense at the time. At the end of the day, choosing 70 had more to do with economics than health.

After a few decades, 70 was considered to a bridge too far for most. So, in 1916, Germany's Reichstag lowered the age to 65 years. In spite of lowering the age, it didn't translate into putting far greater number of elders on the roles of the state pension since average life expectancy was in the late fifties. So once again, the odds of having to pay out were not in the beneficiaries favour.

When other countries began to provide for their own state pensions, they followed Germany's lead and adopted 65 to serve as the qualifying age. For instance, when the United States Congress passed the Social Security Act in 1935, they selected the age of 65. Canada, however, served as somewhat of an outlier. When Parliament passed the Old Age Security Act in 1927, they chose to follow Bismarck's initial proposal and went with 70 years of age to qualify as a beneficiary. Needless to say, average life expectancy in the United States and Canada at the time was hovering around 60 years of age. Even when Canada lowered its qualifying age to 65 years in 1965, the country's average life expectancy was slightly over 70 years.

Setting the retirement age at 65 years, was a sensible choice at the time. It was impossible to know that in under a century, that average life expectancy would be twenty to thirty years beyond anyone's 65th birthday.

What's more, with advances in healthcare, medical treatment and lifestyles, older people are not only living longer healthier lives, but the time in poor health are being pushed back to later years in life. Called the compression of morbidity, this provides an opportunity for people 65 years and over to remain active participants in the labour market for years and even decades longer than they had anticipated.

With people living longer, healthier lives beyond the age of 65, the productive capacity of a society is greatly enhanced. By pushing the proverbial goal posts out farther, more workers can be welcomed into the workforce. More people in the workforce means increased productivity and the potential for greater economic growth.

It seems like society needs a new way to measure age. This is where economics can help. Let's compare the price of a loaf of bread in 1950 to its present day cost in 2019. When making such a comparison, one has to take into account the value of a dollar today versus that same dollar seven decades ago. Inflation has eroded the value of that same dollar. Factoring this in, one comes to a price in what is referred to as current dollars. This means that same loaf of bread which sold for .25 cents in 1950, is priced at $2.75 in 2019.

A similar rule should apply to age. Over the last one hundred years, there has been an increase in life expectancy. For instance, a male born in Canada in 1920, would have a life expectancy of 57 years. That same person born in 1950, could expect to live to 68 years. If that same Canadian was born in 2019, their life expectancy is 86. Over the last one hundred years, the average life expectancy of a Canadian has increased by 30 years.

These extra years are a real game changer. Assuming 65 is the age of retirement, people will need to save far more because they are expecting to live an additional decade. Also, state pension, healthcare and social systems will need to be paid out or provide service for a population that is living longer than was thought possible decades earlier. Therefore, as the purchasing power of money is changed to reflect an increase in prices, so to should chronological age change to reflect increasing life expectancies. This would call for increasing the retirement or old age threshold from its current level of 65, to a much higher value.

Therefore, incenting the population to hang it up at 65 just doesn't make sense any longer. Everyone has heard the phrase, 70 is the new 60 or 60 is the new 50 and so on. Most people today beginning in their mid-60s, are healthier, more active, better educated and wealthier than previous generations. A specific age in one era appears to mean something very different in another. Like the value of money, a mechanism for placing a value on age by adjusting it for increasing life expectancy would prove helpful.

When Bismarck arbitrarily chose 70 as the retirement age over one hundred years ago, even after it was lowered to 65 in 1916, not many were expected to ever live long enough to cash in. Similarly, other countries that chose 65 years believed the same. But that has all changed now with people living far longer. Yet, more than a century later, countries cling to the age of 65, notwithstanding the fact that populations are living on average twenty years longer.

Population aging will lead to one of the most significant transformations in global history. Not only will the basic economic, political and social infrastructure undergo fundamental change, but words and phrases will take on new meaning. This includes, at what age is old considered old?

As a social construct, a person was considered old when they, well, looked old. Societal expectations of old was attributable to someone with gray hair, skin wrinkles and a general physical malaise. These were always sure signs. When healthcare, environmental conditions and lifestyles were more primitive compared to contemporary standards, anyone in their fifties and sixties, certainly in their seventies, would have been considered old.

But, as a social construct, the traditional notion of old, is no longer viable. Advances in cosmetic medical procedures, diet, healthcare and lifestyles, can make age very deceiving. The old adage, *I know it when I see it*, no longer applies. As people live longer healthier lives, what was chronologically considered old in an earlier time, is not today.

Hanging a moniker on people as soon as they reach 65, is not only demeaning and insulting, it is discriminatory. It is dismissing an entire segment of the population just because of their age. Contemporary society should have moved away from these sorts of intolerant notions long ago.

By not embracing 9% of the world's population that is 65 years and over, increasing to 17% by 2050, societies built on foundations of equality of opportunity and social justice, have to ask themselves what kind of society they want. Is it one of exclusion or inclusion? What's more, population aging is not just about *old people*. It is everyone. From the youngest to the oldest. Therefore, at its core, the aging of societies is a debate about values. Namely, freedom, inclusion and common destiny. By segregating people by age, society is on a slippery slope to division, intergenerational friction and widespread poverty.

Increasing longevity has provided for a new stage of life. A stage, however, that is not seen through a lens of opportunity but rather of fear, angst and uncertainty. The questions posed should not be focused on whether any society can *afford* a population that is chronologically older. Concerns as to whether this new age distribution will bankrupt the current system really misses the point.

The focus should rather be on the opportunities this new stage of life offers society. Crafting innovative social programmes supported by the creation of new capacity. Preparing people of all ages for longer lives and the benefits this has for all generations should really be the focus. Not the impending burden the so called, older people will impose.

The use of chronological age as a primary determinant to distinguish between what is old and what is not, is discriminatory in it's effect. When the age distribution skewed younger, age discrimination, although just as real as it is today, did not get much attention. But with the aging of the large baby boom population, it will gather a head of steam that will surely stand as the next big human rights issue. At 64 years and 364 days old, one is considered to be an independent contributing member of society, yet one day later, is not, is patent discrimination. Particularly with increasing numbers of the population living longer, healthier lives decades beyond the so-called retirement age, an arbitrary cut off date when someone is considered to be old, needs to be deemed intolerable. It certainly strikes at the very core values of inclusion, democracy and diversity.

There will not be a single factor that will have such a profound effect on society in the coming years as population aging. Great transformations await. Governments everywhere will need to make some very difficult decisions. These choices will carry a heavy burden. It will be tempting for governments to keep pushing off these changes to some future date for another administration to confront. So rather than being a willing accomplice, populations need to pressure their governments to act now. The current generation has an obligation to those in the future to will them a society that is at least as socially just and inclusive as the one inherited by themselves. Anything less will be a betrayal of the current values of equality of opportunity, social justice and inclusion.

2

The Dynamics Of Population Aging

Buckle up! Brace yourself! Hold on to your seats! Unprecedented and here to stay, the world is on the cusp of great change. The rapidly increasing share of older persons in the population is well on its way to precipitating the most significant demographic transformation in the history of the world. It will have far reaching economic, political and social implications. No one and nothing is immune. Everyone will feel it's sting.

According to data from the United Nations, the global population of those aged 65 years and over is currently estimated to be 8.5% of the world's total population. This was an increase of 150% in the size the 65 plus population from 1980. By 2030, it is projected to increase by more than 60% to 1 billion or 12% of the world's total population. Continuing to increase, by 2050, the 65 plus population will reach 1.6 billion. This will represent 17% of the world's total population. As for specific countries, the data is even more stark. There are currently thirteen countries in the world where those 65 years and over represent at least 20% of their population. By 2050, the number of countries will increase to eighty-two.

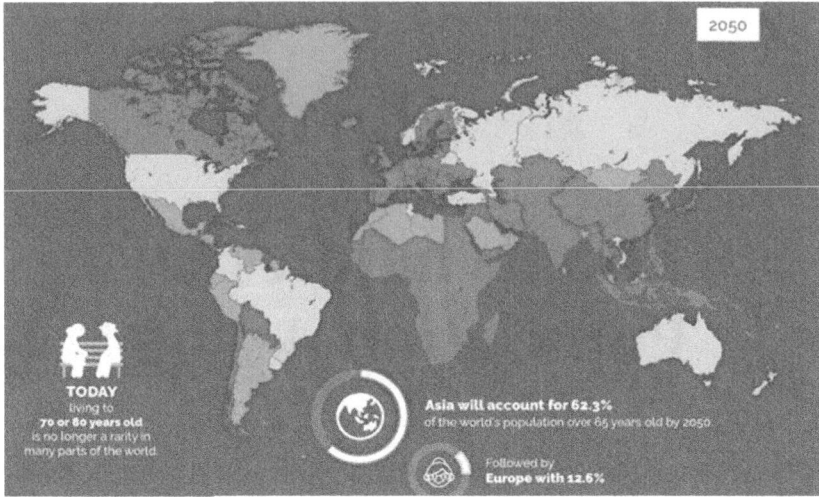

This next comparison will surely set you back on your heels. The global population of persons 65 years and over is growing faster than any other age segment on the globe including youth. In fact, the current number of all those under 20 years of age in the world today is 2.5 billion. By 2050, the number of youth will increase by only 100 million. This is in stark comparison to the rate of growth of those 65+, who will increase over six times the rate of increase the youth population will experience over the identical period of time.

But there's more. If these numbers are of concern, if you are not sitting down, suggest you do so.

February 2019, marked a significant demographic crossing. The global population of those persons 65 years of age and over, for the first time in the history of the world, surpassed the population of everyone on the planet under the age of five years old. This is not a temporary blip. Take a look at the graph below. After the point where the number of 65+ begin to outnumber those five and under, the gap widens. By 2050, it is expected that the population of 65+ will be twice as many as those under five years.

World population

— Population below 5 years old —— Population above 65 years old

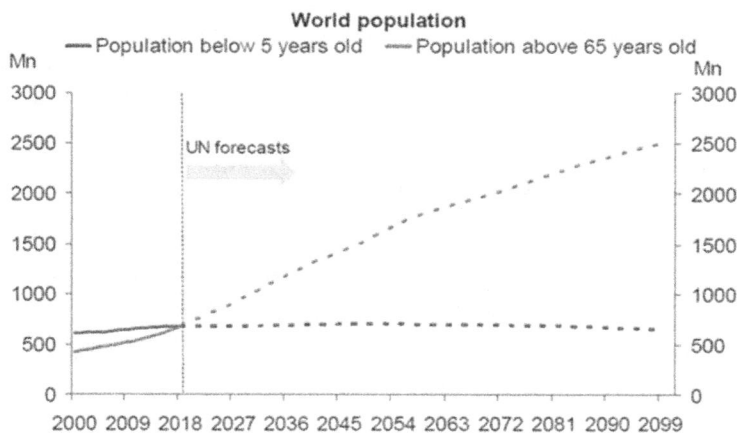

Source: United Nations, Haver Analytics, DB Global Research

The rapid aging of the population is being accelerated by a growing number of persons 80 years and over. In fact, there is no age segment in the world growing faster. Referred to by demographers as the *oldest old*, in 1970, there were 70 million people in the world 80 years of age and over. By 2015, the size of this population increased to 126 million. By 2030, it is projected to grow to 202 million and by 2050, increase to 446 million. In some countries in Asia and South America, the 80+ population is projected to quadruple in size over this same time period.

Many in the younger age cohorts, put the blame for population aging and all the issues associated with it, squarely at the feet of the baby boom generation. Baby boom has become synonymous with greed and self indulgence in many circles. A generation living far beyond its means, they have denied many of the benefits they took and still take for granted, to younger generations. Easy credit made it possible for baby boomers to drive up the price of housing. They are accused of remaining in the workforce longer and thereby reducing employment opportunities for younger generations. Worst of all, they have created a situation where younger generations will be the first ever that will not be financially better off than their parents. This has never occurred before. All the hopes and dreams of every generation that came after the baby boomers have been dashed by this selfish age cohort.

That's how many from generations that have come after the baby boomers would explain how they are having a tougher economic lot. The large baby boom generation drained all the benefits and entitlements for themselves. They have placed their future sustainability in jeopardy. They are responsible for shattering the social contract.

Some of the attacks on the baby boom generation are quite visceral. They are accused of being narcissistic. They are the offspring of the greatest generation. Those who survived the depression and won World War Two. Yet, their children, the baby boomers, spent their teenage years advocating a lifestyle centred around sex, drugs and rock and roll. They made fortunes on Wall Street in the 1980s and even more during the bull market of the 1990s.

Now, they are retiring. For those who have saved enough, they will be fine. But for those who have not, well, they will be living on the backs of the younger working age population. The post baby boom generations fear that increasing taxes and cuts to benefits will provide the revenue to government for old age pensions, healthcare and social programmes. Believing the Great and Just Societies were built by the baby boomers for the baby boomers with little regard for future generations. When it comes time to meet current obligations, lawmakers simply raise the debt ceiling to avert a financial crisis. Let future generations pick up the tab. As a result of their greed and selfishness, they will bestow upon their children, grandchildren and all future generations, record levels of sovereign national debt to pay off. Who cares, say the boomers, it's not my problem.

Baby boomers were the first to bring the world's attention to the need to protect the environment. Yet, they are blamed by younger generations for not doing enough to stop the excesses that have wreaked irreparable harm to the environment that will take generations and and mountains of money to get under control. Younger generations blame the baby boomers for standing by while the environment was systematically destroyed. Waters polluted, deforestation and widespread use of chemicals contaminating lands.

The boomers also get blamed for being the last remanent of racism, sexism and homophobia. Segregating people because of the colour of their skin or barring them from social clubs because of their religious beliefs. The demeaning and appalling fashion how women were treated. Expected to stay at home, objectified as sex symbols or accepting work of equal value but not equal pay. Discrimination against people with different sexual orientation forcing them to pretend to be someone they were not.

Due to their size, influence and excesses, the baby boomers sure do provide a convenient scapegoat. However, nothing could be farther from the truth.

Although the baby boomers have accelerated population aging, they are certainly not to blame for it. The baby boom population is likened to a pig in a python. Once they pass through the snake there will be a return to pre-existing demographic conditions. One big problem with this theory however, population aging started to occur long before even the first baby boomer was a twinkle in their mother's eye.

In the absence of fundamental policy reform, these demographic trends will have profound implications for global economic growth. As the population continues to age, leading to a diminishing number of people in the working age population, productivity will fall. Just like when the baby boom population started to enter the workforce in the 1960s, it boosted the growth potential of economies. However, as the leading edge of the generation is approaching their mid 70s, many either will leave, have left or will reduce their hours in the workforce. Either way, the result will be an economic deceleration and diminished growth.

Although it may seem as if population aging is a fairly recent phenomenon, it has been around for quite some time. Beginning in France in 1865, populations began aging at various times throughout the 20th century. Certainly, countries that began aging recently, are doing so at a far more accelerated pace than those who began doing so far earlier.

The two most dominant conditions for population aging are declining fertility rates and longevity. However, there are some additional sub-factors that also exercise influence. The first of these is the movement of capital and labour. Countries with larger working age populations tend to benefit from large inflows of capital investment. Best example of this was the relocation of large labour intensive manufacturing facilities from the United States to China beginning in the early 1970s.

China's large working age population provided U.S. and other western manufacturing interests a large supply of cheap labour. Lower labour costs helped these companies increase margins and remain competitive on the home front. All this large scale foreign investment led to the creation of a growing middle class in China. It seemed as if a winning formula where everyone was benfitting had been achieved.

However, in an effort to control China's rapidly increasing population, the central government instituted what was referred to as the *One Child Policy*. Beginning in 1979, as the name suggests, couples were restricted to having a single child. The policy did have the desired effect of reducing the number of births in the country.

According to China's National Bureau of Statistics, the country's labour force has been shrinking for years. In 2017, it's working age population, those between the ages of 16 and 59, decreased by more than 5 million. At the same time, the country's population of those 65 years old and over have been on the increase. In 2016, they accounted for 10.8% of the population and in 2017, it increased to 11.4%. China currently has over 158 million people aged 65 and over which has put half of the country's provincial pension funds into deficit and with some running out of money altogether.

Needless to say, it is not everywhere where there is a large working age population there exists large scale capital inflow. In 1952, Africa had a total population of 500,000 million. As of 2019, the population has doubled in size to 1 billion. What's more, 41% of the continent's population is under the age of 15 years. In some countries, half of the population is under the age of 25. Led by Nigeria and Uganda, the two countries with the fastest growing populations, Africa's population is projected to increase to 2.4 billion by 2050. By 2100, Africa's population will reach 4.1 billion accounting for more than 50% of the world's population growth.

Nigeria, which currently has a population of 184 million, is on the verge of a population explosion. It is projected that within two to three generations, Nigeria's population will increase to 1 billion by 2100 making it the third most populous country on earth.

Tanzania, which is currently one of the poorest countries on the planet, has a population of 45 million. The country's population has increased by 11 million in just the last thirteen years. By 2100, Tanzania's population will skyrocket to 276 million.

Massive poverty, lack of education, no family planning. Nigeria and the Democratic Republic of Congo will be home to 40% of Africa's population living in extreme poverty by 2050. There is widespread frustration among Africa's youth due to the limited economic opportunities. Corruption, violence and poor governance are condemning Africa's youth to a future of powerlessness and despair. All the ingredients for large scale social unrest, influence of terrorist groups and criminal behaviour, while all the while watching these countries careen towards becoming failed states.

Needless to say, regardless of the fact that Africa's population is and will increasingly become home to large numbers of young people, given the economic, political and social conditions of most of these countries, the prospect for capital investment currently appears bleak at best. Unlike most African countries, China benefited from foreign capital investment because it not only had a large working age population, but it also possessed strong central governance and effective law enforcement mechanisms. The owners of foreign capital want to know their investments will be protected and therefore will require social stability. This is what China offered and Africa currently does not.

With a growing shortage of both skilled and unskilled workers, a global fight to attract workers is in the beginning throes. Currently, as the economy of the United States is undergoing the kind of growth it has not seen in over fifty years, business of all sizes are expressing concerns over a shortage in the supply of labour. Countries around the world need to take note. As populations age, there will be an ever increasing shortage of both skilled and unskilled workers. This will result in a pitched battle between nations to address domestic shortages.

The movement of young working age people will be a distinctive characteristic of the 21st century. As a result, immigration systems need to undergo fundamental reform. Instead of focusing on family reunification, they need to reorient towards attracting the most skilled and highly educated. As populations age and the working age segment diminishes, if countries want to remain competitive in the global economy, they will need to get in on the hunt for skilled and unskilled workers.

Another dynamic that will influence the shifting age structures of economies in the 21st century, will be movements en masse of young working age people in search of greater economic opportunity. This will be characterized by large groups of migrants leaving their native country due to discrimination, strife and lack of any economic opportunity. According to the United Nations, there is a record high 258 million people worldwide who currently live in a country where they were not born.

The need for additional skilled and unskilled workers, growing global instability and severe weather events as a result of climate change, more people are on the move than ever before. As a result, migration is on the verge of becoming the biggest domestic policy issue for governments. In the United States, immigration reform is currently one of the most bitterly debated partisan issues in the country and promising to even get more intense. Polling indicates that it is also top of mind for Canadians and countries throughout Europe.

Migrants fall into three categories. First, there are those individuals who apply for formal residency status from a country where they currently reside. In other words, they would like to emigrate from their current country and immigrate to another. The second category of migrant is a refugee. As a result of persecution, civil unrest or human rights violations, refugees are individuals who can demonstrate to the country they want admission to that their life will be in danger if they are forced to return. The third type of migrant is the illegal alien. This is the person who has surreptitiously entered a country by circumventing a country's immigration authorities and rules.

Note the large caravans with record numbers of people from all over the world gathering at the U.S. - Mexico border. Armed conflict and civil unrest in Syria. Large boat loads of people from Africa arriving at Europe's southern coast. In recent years, these are the large movements of people that have garnered international attention. The record numbers of migrants at the U.S. border with Mexico has reached historic levels. Most agree that it is a humanitarian crisis but any possibility of it coming to a reasonable resolution anytime soon is unlikely. Currently bogged down in the hyper partisan swamp of U.S. politics it will also need to be part of reforming the country's immigration system.

Large numbers of migrants who arrived at Europe's shores over the past few years have not been deemed to be legitimate refugees. The countries where they are currently resident have been attempting to return them to the first country in Europe where the asylum seeker first arrived. This has resulted in a growing number of squabbles between European Union member states as to who is responsible for the deportees. Greece has refused to accept most of the transfer requests from Germany and Hungary has refused to accept any.

Migration is a zero sum. The gain of one country or region is at the loss of another. However, large scale migration can have the effect of altering demographic patterns since migrants overwhelmingly skew younger. Long trips taken by migrants are not for the faint of heart. Bottom line is, the vast majority of these migrants are honest, hard working people. Some are skilled and some are not.

Regardless, with populations in the world's poorest countries poised to jump from its current size of 954 million to 3.2 billion by 2100, developed countries would be well advised to work with others in the international community and bring these countries out of their current poverty traps. Doing so would put them on a surer economic, social and political footing but most importantly, secure global stability.

The challenge for developed countries in the coming decade will be to manage the flow of young, educated and skilled workers from areas with younger populations to replace their own diminishing workforces. Regions where younger populations are increasing can serve as a stable reservoir of potential workers so sorely needed in the developed world. Countries who want to maintain or increase their competitive edge would be well advised to pay close attention to these dynamics of the shifting demography not only in their own countries, but around the world.

3

Why Population Aging Matters

It may not feel like it now, but population aging is poised to become the most consequential event of the century. Unprecedented and permanent, population aging will impact every conceivable aspect of society. What's more, they go far beyond fiscal policy considerations.

Significant policy changes will be required. The extent of these changes however, will depend on how far current policy makers decide to distribute it's economic burdens across generations.

As the population ages, the workforce diminishes leading to less revenue for the government. Governments are then left with some very difficult choices to make. They can increase existing taxes or impose new ones. Or, they can reduce spending on current age related programmes or shift resources from other policy envelopes or any combination of these. Another way is, of course, is to increase spending.

Increased spending is the least painful way a government can fund programmes today without having to burden themselves with paying the cost now. It's akin to going out with your family to the finest restaurant in town. You all order the most expensive dishes on the menu. Desert? Of course. No need to hold back. But when the cheque comes, the dad says, I would normally put this charge on my credit card, but it's maxed out. Not to worry, though. My grandchildren come by in twenty years and will pay you then. Just put it on their tab and they will take care of it. How do you think that would go over? You and the rest of the family would be in the kitchen scrubbing dishes before you can say, Howdy Doody.

So much for intergenerational fairness. Notwithstanding the restaurant management, can't imagine this person's grandchildren would be too thrilled about footing the tab for a meal they had no part of enjoying themselves. Perhaps though, if half of the bill been paid, the resentment would be less than if none of it was paid. But these are choices the grandchildren have no part in making. The decisions were made for them.

The same with government. The choices governments make today are not just about the here and now. They have implications for future generations. So, just like the family who could have decided to forgo the expensive restaurant meal for a much cheaper fast food dinner, government faces similar decisions about whether to spend or not to spend. By not spending as much of the money they have currently have on hand on themselves, they or putting large expenses on their credit card, they could choose to indulge less and thereby willing more to their children and grandchildren. By opting for a more thrifty alternative, they may find solace in the knowledge that by making a small sacrifice now, their grandchildren will have more resources at their disposal in the future if they have the need.

A stable and prosperous economy will depend a lot on how much confidence the public has in the knowledge that promised benefits will be delivered. This applies to both the current and future generations. It's a fine line governments are required to toe. Sacrifices by the current generation will be required. They will either have to consume less or work more or both. If not, future generations will need to pay the bill. What this all boils down to is how much the current generation is prepared to sacrifice for their children, grandchildren, great grandchildren and so on. After all, future generations are not here to speak for themselves.

In fairness and in the spirit of intergenerational equity, the burden should be spread equally across generations. Passing the burden on down the generational line will mean higher taxes and less benefits later. Ask any parent if they would be in favour of burdening their own children and grandchildren with higher taxes, less programme benefits and a weaker economy. Chances are one would be hard pressed to find anyone who would be in favour.

Bottom line is governments need to resist the temptation to increase deficits. As the working age population diminishes and revenue to government decreases, governments will need to make some pretty difficult choices. Naturally, any government would prefer to lower taxes. Hard to imagine a political party getting much support among the electorate by promising to increase taxes. Other efficiencies will need to be found.

To achieve intergenerational equity, current governments need to exercise fiscal prudence. But that's not the only reason for doing so. Ratcheting up one deficit after another will compound sovereign debt. In the event of a economic crisis, a large deficit and debt do not leave the government with very much fiscal space in which to respond effectively. Depending on the amount of fiscal room available to a government will dictate how aggressively it can respond to a crisis by way of tax reductions or spending increases.

Studies have shown that the greater the national debt the less effective their response will be to any crisis. Any country with a high debt, as Greece, Portugal, Spain and Italy demonstrated in the last decade, will be be forced to pay high interest rates in the sovereign debt markets due to their higher than average risk of paying it back. In addition, as a condition of any bail out, the country may be subject to abrogating complete control of their own government's fiscal policy.

This is what makes reform of healthcare and social benefit programmes such a priority. With a diminishing working age population, the funding of these benefit programmes will come to rely more and more on deficit spending. That is why any change to these programmes must include strengthening national saving and additional measures to reduce the burden on future generations to pay for the excesses of the current one.

As unprecedented numbers of people age into their 60s, 70s, and more, societies are facing record level shortfalls in retirement savings. Assuming most people in the developed world will support themselves in retirement by at least one of the following: Government provided pension, a defined benefit or defined contribution plan provided by a former employer, and/or their savings, each one is under increasing strain.

Certainly longer life expectancies need to be celebrated. But with longer lives comes an increasing cost to the years in retirement. The current retirement savings gap, that is the shortfall in pension savings, for the world's largest pension markets is $70 trillion. As many find it increasingly challenging to save for retirement, low levels of financial literacy and lack of access to savings vehicles, there will be a large number of people who will have a sufficient amount of savings.

In 2015, The World Economic Forum conducted a study of eight countries to determine current retirement savings gaps and their growth over the forthcoming three and a half decades. What they found was astonishing. Based on their projections, the retirement savings gap will increase from it's current amount of $70 trillion, to $400 trillion by 2050. Each day for the coming three decades, $28 billion of additional deficit will be added.

The pension challenge currently confronting the world is unprecedented in scope and nature. What's more, with no solution in sight, it is expected to grow only worse.

Further exacerbating these challenges is the pace at which population aging is occurring. Remember France became the first aging society in 1865. To get some perspective, it would take another 130 years before it became an aged society when those 65 and over would outnumber the segment of the population under sixteen. Now, compared to Japan, the most rapidly aging population on earth, they went from having the youngest population in the G7 in 1960, to having the oldest population in the world by 2008. They have retained this title ever since.

For Japan to transition from an aging to an aged society took one-third of the time it took France. But compared to some of the other countries who are currently aging, such as South Korea, Japan's timeline pales in comparison. South Korea became an aging society in 1999. It became aged in 2017. That's a little more than one-third of the time it took Japan.

According to Moody's, one of the world's leading credit rating agencies, 60% of the countries they rate are currently aging. Moody's also has a more exclusive club of countries where at least 20% of their population is 65 and over. By 2020, there will be thirteen countries in this group and by 2030 the numbers will swell to 34. Two countries leading the list will be South Korea, whose 65+ population will reach 38% and Japan still ranking first at 40%.

Although Japan still comes in as the reigning champion in terms of countries with the oldest population, the title for the fastest aging population goes to South Korea. What took France almost 145 years to reach and Japan 50 years, South Korea will accomplish this feat in under three decades.

The speed at which country's are currently aging is giving rise to a rather grim prospect. With a fertility rate currently of 1.05 children per woman, well below the 2.1 required to serve as a stable replacement value, there is the possibility that South Korea's population could cease to exist by 2750.

A study conducted by South Korea's National Assembly Research Service in 2014, based on that year's fertility rate of 1.19, the country's current population of 50 million will decline to 40 million by 2056. The simulation model projects outward that by 2100, the population will decline to 20 million and by 2136, the population of South Korea will drop even further to 10 million. The study concludes that by 2750, the last South Korean will die making it the first national group in the world to become extinct.

Japan is on the same track as South Korea. A similar study undertaken by Japan's Tohoku University in 2012, concluded that based on current demographic trends, they project that the last Japanese baby will be born in 3011.

The extinction of a national population due to aging is naturally the worst case scenario caused by population aging. Keep in mind, these are projections, not predictions. Even if it were to occur, it is a long way off into the future and presumably countries confronted with the possibility of such a scenario would take action well in advance in an effort to boost its fertility rate. If not, South Korea, Japan and others could potentially face the unthinkable possibility of national extinction.

Although these are just projections, they need to be taken very seriously. After all, they are based on current demographic trends and if one thing is for sure, demography has an inherent determinism. To say such a scenario is far off in the future so no need to be concerned about it now, would be repeating the same mistake countries are currently committing. Ignoring rapidly changing demographics now will simply impose greater hardships on society later. Best for governments to be proactive and thereby maintain a semblance of control. By throwing up their hands and waiting to see what cards are dealt, is a mug's game.

Picture this ... shifting demographics are like a runaway locomotive heading downhill. It starts off slowly but as it lurches forward it begins to pick up a head of steam. With each revolution of it's wheels it moves faster and faster. Soon the speed at which it is travelling will make it too difficult and then ultimately just impossible to stop. But, if it's not at least slowed down, it will careen out of control and wreak havoc and devastation for everyone at the bottom of the hill who are unaware of its approach.

Population aging will pose a host of challenges that governments will need to confront much sooner rather than later. Analysts all agree that increasing longevity and declining fertility rates will have a profound impact on all aspects of society. But as the aging of the population rapidly accelerates, the window of opportunity for governments to act will soon slam shut.

Yet, in spite of the fact that populations have been aging for decades, some even longer, governments have done little to much of anything to facilitate as much of a seamless transition as possible to an aged society. Quite the contrary, when government's need to act, they have done so by transfusing money into existing transfer models. Sure increasing the size of budgets are a lot easier than wholesale reform of the system through the building of new capacity. But, by committing more money to a model that is no longer functioning in the way it was intended to do so because the configuration of the population has changed, is only dangerously postponing significant decisions that should be made now.

When developed countries had large working age populations, demographics worked in favour of current transfer models. Governments and economies benefited from the increased growth known as a demographic dividend. But as populations age, workforces shrink leading to productivity and competitiveness challenges. The once *demographic dividend* now changes to a *demographic tax*. According to the Organisation for Economic Cooperation and Development, over the coming decades, the demographic tax will slow growth and increase income inequality.

So what are the current set of options available to government?

The most common and go-to policy option are tax increases. In addition to the income tax, payroll deductions at source, there are a raft of others that can be increased. There are specific taxes that apply to retail sales, services, gasoline, cigarette, marijuana, insurance, realty, just to name a few. Nevertheless, in spite of all these taxes, governments everywhere run budgetary deficits but more significantly, are carrying ever increasing levels of sovereign debt.

As the population ages, government expenditures will increase. With fewer taxpayers, there is less revenue. Fewer workers lead to a smaller economy.

In addition, for most who are 65 years and over, the data has shown that their patterns of consumption decline. This is presumably a result of being on a fixed income with less disposable income.

Studies also show that as people age, their purchase of products such as cigarettes and alcohol decrease. So, not only are there fewer working age paying income tax, but there are a growing number of older members of the population reducing their consumption of products linked to products and services with high rates of tax. Governments get hit with a double whammy.

As the population ages, the pool of working age people (16 to 64) diminishes in relation to the non-working population 65 years and over. In Canada, the dependency ratio, as it is called, has fallen from a robust 9 workers for every one person 65 years and over in 1960 and a further drop to 4.7 to 1 in 2016. As population aging accelerates, the ratio will drop to 2.5 to 1 by 2030.

The tightening old age dependency ratio is not good news for Canada. A reduction in the size of available workers means fewer taxpayers which translate into a decrease in the revenues governments can raise. This results in less monies available for health-care, Old Age Security and other age related and non-age related expenditures.

When an economy has a diminishing workforce, the main consequence is a drop in the standard of living for everyone. Fewer workers will need to be more productive to make up for any loss on this front. Doing more with fewer workers will require large capital investment in new and advanced machinery and equipment. But productivity growth has been a recurrent challenge for many in the G7, including Canada, in recent years. Adding an aging population to the mix puts increasing downward pressure on productivity leading to decreasing innovation and an economy where everyone will need to get used to having less.

For business, the availability of workers both skilled and un-skilled will become increasingly challenging to attract. Historically, this has not been considered to be much of a problem. There was enough talent to satisfy the demand. But now, with more work than there are availability of workers to fill these positions, workers become free agents, or mercenaries, for sale to the highest bidder. Human capital, rather than natural resources, will be the key to future prosperity. Businesses will now be joined by governments in trying to attract and retain both skilled and unskilled workers.

Attracting human capital will be tied in to the reformation of immigration systems. This needs to be a top priority for developed countries. Currently favouring family reunification, immigration systems must focus on attracting new immigrants with skills. Particularly those who possess the knowledge to function effectively in the information technology age.

A function of the industrial age, bilateral and multilateral instruments such as, free trade and foreign investment protection agreements, were used to protect manufacturing workers. However, with a diminishing pool of younger workers in the pipeline, countries currently on top and want to stay there and those who want to join them, will need to fight tooth and nail for the world's limited number of highly skilled workers. Those countries in the hunt should be pushing for free trade in human capital. Brain power, in an age of rapidly advancing technology, should be able to move more freely between countries via free trade zones for workers to gravitate to where they are needed most.

Current systems that place restrictions on foreign trained professionals need to be brought into the 21st century. Take Canada, for instance, where the country's interprovincial trade barriers pose significant challenges to the free movement of labour from one province to another. These restrictions are archaic and need to be modernized and not used as a tool to restrict the supply of the number of trained professionals who can practice in the field.

As populations age, cost of healthcare rise, pension liabilities become dangerously underfunded and all other age related transfers, come under increasing financial pressures. A diminishing working age population and a shrinking tax base mean less government revenue. To meet both current and future expenditure commitments, governments will be facing increasing financial stress. The great social policy achievements of the 20th century embodied in what is euphemistically referred to as, the welfare state, will have their very sustainability placed in jeopardy. Old age security, public pensions, healthcare and a host of other age related social services are just some. Meeting growing funding requirements of these programmes today, governments will need to shift resources away from areas such as education, training, infrastructure and more, and thereby sacrificing future generations. It's like the old Popeye cartoon where Wimpy orders a hamburger to eat today but will not be able to pay for it until next week.

Some governments play these kinds of dangerous games. With a diminishing number of younger persons in a population and a burgeoning number of older people, some governments will borrow from Paul to pay Peter. In other words, move funding from programmes for the young to sustain initiatives for those over 65. For instance, cut education to pay for very costly new healthcare technology. Both are necessary and needed. Any kind of solution must not be one where a choice is made at the expense of another generation. To do so would surely put a society on the fast track to gross social inequality and intergenerational friction.

To make the transition to and become a successful aged society, there must be policies in place that speak to the collective welfare of the population. Only through the development of new capacity can this be achieved. Certainly not policy choices that will pit one segment of the population against another.

The future costs of these programmes are so staggering its boggles the imagination. To keep kicking this can down the road, as many a government are want to do, will result in nothing less than their implosion. What even makes this situation worse, is that it is the developed countries are on the front lines of these demographic changes. For any one of these nations to fall victim to these pressures will spread like a dye cast in a pool of water with the same ability to stop its advance. There are not enough creditors in the world to cover a debt of such proportions.

The world's shifting demographics pose unprecedented challenges to the fiscal and macroeconomic stability of the global economy. For some countries, such as Japan, the effects have been felt for some time now and will only grow more intense. For the others, well, they are all on borrowed time. Some have more time to spare than others. But, regardless of how much time any government currently has, economies are so intricately interweaved, the ripples of economic discontent have the ability to move across vast oceans and land masses in the blink of an eye. Governments are now coming under increasing pressure from others to develop a strategic plan of action on how to meet these challenges. The government of Japan, the host country for the 2019 G20 meetings, has placed population aging on the agenda for discussion by the leaders. Japan, more than most other countries, understand that governments cannot eat their cake and have it too. There is no time to waste.

4

It's The Demography, Stupid!

How old are you today? Now, how old will you be one year from today? Yes, one year older. That's correct It's called demographic forecasting. Pretty reliable, isn't it.

Throughout history, demographic change took place slowly and predictably. Plodding along at glacial speed. Change occurred over long periods of time. But, as long as the population pyramid approximated a triangle, where the number of younger people outnumbered older age segments, there was really no reason to pay much attention. With all those under 65 years of age far outnumbering those over it and those under seventeen years greater than those between 18 and 64 years, no need to fix what wasn't broken.

However, the pace of population aging has accelerated in recent decades. Unlike France, which took well over a century to become an aged society, a combination of plummeting fertility levels, longevity, high levels of emigration of young people and more deaths than births, some countries are aging at break neck speed. Nevertheless, most governments are reacting to the rapid changes in the distribution of the population as if there was not much change at all.

Much has been written about change. People don't like it, organizations try to avoid it and governments attempt delaying a response until they are out of other options. Given that no one likes change, the larger the organization the more difficult it is to alter course. One thing for sure. Government is big. In most developed countries, it is the first or second largest employer. An entity of that size, by it's very nature, would be very difficult to change it's ways. After all, it is even said that one can't teach an old dog new tricks. So just imagine trying to change the culture of an organization with 275,000 employees, as in the case of Canada, or 2.8 million who work for the United States government. No easy task.

Due to it's sheer size, no one has ever accused government of maneuvering with cat like agility. So it's understandable that in the case of responding to the challenges posed by population aging that government would answer the call with the speed one would expect from a sloth on valium. Slow and incremental shifts that are ultimately going to require significant policy responses are usually better left to the next government.

Nevertheless, governments do have strong track records of stepping up and acting quickly when necessary. In times of war, natural disaster or patriotic fervor, governments have been successful in rallying it's population quickly and effectively. These instances, however, have been few and far between.

On the other hand, business is typically quicker to catch on and changes in demography are no exception. After all, whether they are selling products or services, they always want what they have to offer to be purchased. If not, the business offering these products or services, will not be around very long.

The business graveyard is certainly littered with the names of large retailers or service providers who over the years not paid close enough attention to demographic changes within their own marketplace. Eaton's, Gimbels, Sears, Pan Am, Blockbuster and F.W. Woolworth, just to name a few. Many were dominant in their category. However, lack of attention to changing demographics by way of poor marketing, bad locations or failing to keep up to date with customer demand, is a recipe for disaster. Lack of close attention to demographic change will cause the customer base to fall out from below. The question that everyone who has something to sell should constantly be asking themselves is: How big is my current market and is it getting bigger? At the end of the day, demographics are all about counting people and discerning trends.

Demographics are also well known to political parties seeking office. Parties craft platforms they believe will appeal to enough voters to get them elected. Although based on the political party's ideological beliefs, these platforms are typically the result of painstaking polling, consultation and focus group analysis. The objective is to offer policies that will excite their own party's base and be attractive to enough to broker enough of those voters who are not partisans to support their position on issues.

The use of demographics for political parties differ from that of business. Success for a political candidate is garnering one more vote than their nearest rival. Naturally, they strive for a greater plurality, but the victory is the same whether its by a single vote or by 10,000 votes.

Business on the other hand, is not, and should not, be satisfied with selling one more product than their closest competition. Their goal is to sell as many of their products as possible and hope their competition sells as few as their own products as possible. Their overall objective is to dominate the marketplace or category group. In other words, manufacturer A produces 1 million boxes of detergent. Manufacturer B produces an identical amount. Sure manufacturer A would be delighted to sell a few boxes more than manufacturer B. However, for manufacturer A to dominate their market they would want to sell a lot more of their own product or be the 1st choice of the overwhelming majority of consumers. Keeping a close eye on the changing demographics of consumers who purchase, and do not purchase, for that matter, detergent, will be key to a manufacturer's success.

The central question for any business, government, political party, urban planner, or anyone involved in strategic planning, is the following:

1. How big is the current market?
2. Has it been increasing or decreasing in size to this point in time.
3. Does the customer match the current or changing demography?
4. What is the time frame for any demographic changes?

Although demography is about counting up numbers, it is also about trends. Extrapolating vital information from a mass of data and massaging it until discernible strategic directions emerge. It's similar to that far overused cliché coined by hockey great, Wayne Gretzky: *You want to skate to where the puck is going, not where it has been.*

Once all the data has been culled, a demographic story emerges. The intricacies of this story will be pieced together like a big jigsaw puzzle. Once complete, it will explain how a city, region, country, customer base, or the world, is changing over time. There are many applications, permutations and functions that are offered. Demographic data will provide insights into the changing dynamics of people, populations and manners of behaviour. These sets of data can be used to identify patterns and predict future demand or lack thereof. The information can be used spatially to highlight specific patterns or can be used to make a solid case for investment or to base strategic business or investment decisions upon.

Any government or business that ignores demographic changes, does so at their own peril. A recent example of a business that ignored demographic developments and ended up paying the price for doing so, was Toys R' US (USA).

Founded in 1948, their timing could not have been better. Established at the cutting edge of the baby boom, Toys R' Us (USA) was a destination retail outlet for not only members of that generation but also their children. By the mid 1990s, Toys R' Us (USA) rode this demographic wave to become one of the most popular retail outlets in North America.

But by the mid 2000s, Toys R Us (USA) began to struggle. In late 2017, it filed for Chapter 11 bankruptcy protection. By early 2018, all 750 stores across the United States closed for last time. This is in spite of the fact that the US National Retail Association projected that holiday retail sales for 2018 would come in at $720 billion representing a 4.8% increase increase from the year before.

So the question is: How could a major toy retailer, a mainstay of the US marketplace, not survive in what was shaping up to be the best consumer market in over a decade?

For the answer, one does not have to go much further than the company's 2017 annual filing where it cited declining birth rates in the United States as a threat to sales. The report states:

Most of our end-customers are newborns and children and, as a result, our revenues are dependent on the birth rates in countries where we operate. In recent years, many countries' birth rates have dropped or stagnated as their population ages, and education and income levels increase. A continued and significant decline in the number of newborns and children in these countries could have a material adverse effect on our operating results.

Clearly, Toys R Us (USA) fortunes would rise or fall with the size of its target market.

Going back to the four questions every retailer should be asking themselves:

1. How big is the current market?
2. Has it been increasing or decreasing in size to this point in time
3. Does the customer match the current or changing demography?
4. What is the time frame for any demographic changes?

Toys R' US (USA) serves as a poster child for not paying close enough attention to demographics. The reason for its growing success beginning in 1948, was the cause of its downfall in 2017. Indeed, if anyone took the time to take a look at demographic trends long before they became so evident, it would have been clear as day that the drop in revenue was a result of fewer children.

But Toys R' US (USA) has not been the only retailer to shutter it's operations recently for precisely the same reasons. There were others who did not pay close enough attention to the changing demographics in the marketplace. The Children's Place closed 300 of its 1,014 stores in 2018, and Gymboree, a clothing retailer for children shuttered all their 490 stores across North America. Other retailers who closed their doors in 2018, including Sears, Kmart, Brookstone, and many other well known names, did not rely on the children's market, but nevertheless did not pay close enough attention to demogaphic changes within their own category, suffered the same fate.

There are many lessons to be learned from the Toys R' US (USA) experience with respect to demographics. Specific indicators should have been apparent to Toys R Us (USA). For instance, the data showed that more women have been entering the workforce over the past two decades. These same women have been either putting off having children or deciding not to have children at all. Millennials, the generation born between the years 1980 to 2000, the data shows they been choosing career over children due mostly to large outstanding student loans. This generation is also eager to gain financial independence from their parents.

One other significant demographic Toys R Us (USA) should have been aware of. Since 1990, the incidence of teen pregnancies has been falling considerably. This is due to increased levels of sex education in schools and increased access and use to contraception. Remember, demographics tell a story. Each set of data is piece of the puzzle. One piece is just as important as every other to complete the full puzzle and get a whole picture.

It appears as if it was not just one set of sexecitives at Toys R Us (USA) who were not paying attention to the shifting demographics. The company installed a new CEO in 2000, followed by an expensive re-launch. Nevertheless, the chain still floundered.

Rather than paying attention to the ongoing changes in demographics, the company's new CEO blamed competition from other retailers to explain why revenues were down. To further compound matters, Toys R Us (USA) also operated some 500 Babies R Us outlets across the United States. For the identical reasons revenues were down for the parent company, Babies R Us just put a further drag on reveunes.

It turned out, however, that Toys R Us (USA) wasn't the only one not paying much attention to the demographic changes. Even after closing its Kids R Us outlets in 2004, which the company had operated for two decades, on March 17, 2005, a consortium of investment firms consisting of Bain Capital Partners, Kohlberg Kravis Roberts and Vornado Realty Trust, announced a $6.6 billion leveraged buyout of Toys R Us (USA) and took the company private. They further doubled down in 2009 with the purchase of the iconic New York City toy store, FAO Schwarz.

The new owners announced they would be opening additional stores around the United States including some as large superstores. In 2014, they announced, what's they called, a *TRU Transformation Strategy*. Under this plan, they planned to focus on foundational issues affecting future growth. These included a closer integration of their online and retail business, promotions, less cluttered aisles and an attempt to offer an overall better customer experience.

Yet, in spite of the strategy, Toys R Us (USA) filed for Chapter 11 bankruptcy in September 2017. In some cases, changing demographics may catch a business that is just not paying attention. What makes the Toys R' Us (USA) example stand out as it does, is that they knew all along that it was changing demographics that was causing the plunge in revenues. One has to wonder where the Board of Directors were while these life and death decisions for the business which in turn raises serious governance issues. It seems like no one, from the Board of Directors, through the executive, to management, were aware in the slightest of the shifting demographics and the impact it would have on the future of the toy business.

It wasn't until 2017, that the company acknowledged in their Annual Report that demographics were to blame for the demise of the business. Toys R' Us (USA) should serve as a case study of the importance of being aware of demographic trends and the effect they will have on the future of the business. Notwithstanding the fact that it was as plain as day in the 2017 company annual filing. Someone in the company knew.

Credit where credit is due. There are examples of businesses who have done their demographic homework and it certainly shows. Since 2015, Amazon has been working on developing technologies for the older population. According to a 2016 report conducted by U.S. based, *Aging In Place Technology Watch*, they reported that the marketplace to assist older adults is expected to increase from its current level of $2 billion to well over $30 billion within coming years. The increase is largely due to more people choosing to age at home.

Amazon Alexa, a virtual assistant, is capable of voice interaction, making to-do lists, voice activated phone calls, providing reminders, news, sports, traffic and weather, and a host of other applications. The device has a multitude of healthcare applications that are currently just scratching the surface.

Amazon's purchase of PillPack, an internet pharmacy that packages prescription medicines for users who suffer from chronic ailments, also demonstrates that someone at the company is paying very close attention to the aging demographics. Designed to capture the growing mail order prescription market, PillPack is gong to head to head and competing with pharmacy giant CVS and Walmart for the rapidly increasing prescription drug market.

The purchase of Whole Foods by Amazon in 2017, is also a key component of the company's strategy to serve the aging baby boomer marketplace. Home delivery of groceries is a burgeoning business and puts them head to head with Walmart and Costco. Walmart has even teamed up with Google to offer voice ordering capability.

There are a multitude of companies and businesses who are paying close attention to the swiftly changing demography. Those who develop a sound strategy around the aging of the population and changing consumer demands and preferences, will end up in the winner's circle.

Companies, however, who think they can sell to the baby boom market simply by creating an older version of their product, will fail. Perhaps in the past, products that were designed to appeal to an older segment of the population had some appeal. But this strategy will not work with the baby boomers.

Remember, the baby boom generation is used to having things done their way. Individualized and personalized. This new generation of *old* is not the traditional notion of the senior citizen quietly fading into the background. Baby boomers are healthier and more active than any generation that has come before them. They have no intention of slowing down as they age.

Products and services that seek out the lowest common denominator, just won't cut it with the baby boom generation. Products designed and made for elderly members of the population in the past, will fail. Plain, ugly and institutional, products that scream, Hey!, I'm old!, is not for a generation that will never be caught saying: 'I've fallen and I can't get up'. They may wear such a device if it resembles an attractive piece of jewelry, but they will certainly not wear a big white panic button around their neck.

For those who understand the significance of the current demographic shift and adjust to it, they will reap great success. However, for those who do not, well, they will join the other businesses and services to commiserate about what could have been, if only they had paid attention to demographics.

The use of demographics provide the most reliable tool for forecasting the future. Yet, they are underappreciated. Why? Well, that's anyones guess. But it's puzzling why more use is not made of this treasure trove of invaluable information. Demographics hold the answers to many of the current unknowns for both business and government. They can reveal whether a particular product will sell or how many schools need to be built. Not insignificant items.

The most important feature of demographics is the ability to discern how a country's economy will perform. The age structure of a population can reveal whether a country's economy will prosper or stagnate. Demographics are powerful. There are no data sets more important than demographics. Governments and business need to stand up and take more notice of the invaluable information they can offer. Need answers? Look to the demographics.

5

Demography Is Destiny

*D*emography is destiny, a phrase first attributed to French sociologist and philosopher Auguste Comte is as relevant today as it was in 1880. There is no more reliable tool to plan for the future than demographics.

Anyone currently residing in an urban area built up before the mid 1960s, there is no doubt at least three or four buildings nearby that at one time served as public schools. Still standing today, most of these buildings have been repurposed.

Why so many schools? Well, let's take a look at demographics for the explanation. Canada, for instance, in 1949, there were 2.4 million students enrolled across the country in elementary schools. By 1959, the number of students had swelled to over 4 million. Simply put, additional schools needed to be built to accommodate this massive wave of students.

Aware that the existing school stock would not nearly be enough, school boards across the country took the decision to build additional schools. The demographics in this instance were easy to read. It was a no-brainer. Constructed primarily in new sub-divisions, these schools were usually built adjacent to parks, community centres, shopping and strip plazas. Parks and community centres were to be used by all those rapidly growing number of young families in these neighbourhoods. The kids would swim in the community pool, families would attend carnivals, the parent's lodge annual picnic would be held on one of those hot sunny Sunday July afternoons. No sunscreen or cleaning up your garbage after you left either. Park crews would come by after and pick all that up. For all the boys and girls, the community centre and park would also be used for the local meetings of the scouts and guides.

Emerging from two decades of record low births, no one anticipated that the end of the war would usher in twenty years of an unprecedented number of births. The shifting demographic landscape quickly became clear for all to see. At that point, demographics took over. It soon became evident that much more of everything would be needed.

It didn't take long to figure out that schools, hospitals, and infrastucture would be necessary to accommodate this explosion in the population. Naturally, no one would be able to anticipate how long these record number of births would keep going. What they did know, however, was that all these births year after year would eventually mean a record number of teens, young adults and adults. Policy makers and industry knew that change was necessary to accommodate the increase in the population. What's more, there was no time to wait. They needed to act quickly.

Policy makers were charged with building the apparatus and infrastructure for the new economy. Government coffers were flush with money. A post war economy that was undergoing a massive economic boom was generating unprecedented levels of government revenue. All that pent up demand during the war years seemed to explode as soon as the allies defeated the axis powers. Record numbers of births augered well for a future filled with continued prosperity. Every new born represented a future tax payer, another worker and greater productivity. What's more, there seemed to be no end on the horizon.

Similarly, for companies with a product to sell, the timing could not have been better. Imagine those in the diaper, baby products and toy businesses. They were riding high at the peak of a demographic wave that had no end in sight. It felt as if gail force winds must have been at their backs that only seemed to get stronger with each passing year.

The demographic trends were easy enough to read. A large number of births translated into a swelling at the base of the population pyramid. This is the perfect population configuration. A large and young population to support the far fewer in number older age cohorts above them. Good times lay ahead. Government was well positioned to lavish the population with big ticket spending programmes. The foundation of the *Just Society* in Canada and the *Great Society* in the United States were firmly in place. Even more, it would still be another three to four decades until the baby boomers would reach their peak earning years. During this time, governments at all levels were smacking their lips at all the money they had at their disposal to spend.

By the early part of the 1950s, cities in Canada and the United States underwent a massive building blitz. Everything from health and educational facilities, community centres, and new and expanding infrastructure projects were undertaken. The Trans Canada Highway, the U.S. Interstate Highway system, subway construction and the St. Lawrence Seaway, were just some of the massive expenditures undertaken at the time. The economy was booming with exuberance and government was eager to build and invest in the growth and expansion. As this generation grew into their teens, additions to and the creation of new university campuses were constructed. Community colleges burst on to the scene beginning in the late 1960s. By 1973, Ontario alone had twenty-two community colleges.

It was not just government that went on a spending spree during these decades. Industry also followed the demographic trend lines and saw that there was lots of money to be made. First and foremost, where were all these burgeoning families going to live? As the number of births after the Second World War continued to grow, by the early 1950s, cities like Toronto was running out livable urban space. Not to be denied, urban areas were expanded to the north, east, west and south.

Pioneered in the United States, William Levitt, a home builder, envisioned new planned communities that would house returning veterans. These homes would be built with speed, efficiency and cost effective construction. In 1948, the construction of new homes were being turned out as if they were coming off an assembly line. Materials were all pre-cast and pre-cut. Mostly required just assembly by all the sub-contractors that were employed. The workers on the job sites were paid well so the very homes they were constructing they could also afford to purchase. On average, each home had a list price of $8,000 ($85,000 2019) and came equipped with modern kitchen appliances. That meant refrigerators, no more iceboxes.

Similarly, in Canada, E.P. Taylor, the owner of O'Keefe Breweries, could also count. Seeing the increasing number of births, he purchased 2,000 acres of land at the northern tip of Toronto. Taylor envisioned the new development as a community. Long and winding roads, parks, schools and a local shopping centre. The homes were built to house the growing number of young families who were living in close quarters in the city's core. The concept was that these homes, affordable in price, would be purchased by those members of the growing middle class. Historically, people had to live near where they worked. However, with the affordability of automobiles, people could now drive to work.

The phrase shopping mall was added to the lexicon. Large developers who saw the exodus of young families from the inner city to the suburbs, knew they would need a convenient place to shop for groceries, clothes and furniture. Bringing all the big name retailers, restaurants and amenities such as movie theatres and bowling alleys all placed it all under one roof. The shopping mall is born.

Developers weren't the only ones to see these migration patterns. Working hand in hand with developers, were the large department store chains such as Eaton's, Simpsons, and the Hudson's Bay Company, also recognized this vast opportunity. Historically anchored at the main downtown intersections in Canada's cities, they now saw the suburbs as their new frontier for growth. Polo Park in Winnipeg and Yorkdale in Toronto, were constructed to serve as regional shopping centres for the quickly growing numbers of suburban residents. Highway exits would funnel cars right into shopping mall parking lots.

Within climate controlled environments, shoppers were protected from the frigid and howling winds of harsh winters. Similarly, air conditioning in the summer months provided a comfortable day for shopping, lunch and an afternoon movie matinee with the kids. As these malls began to dot the expanding suburban landscape, venturing downtown was no longer necessary other than to see the Christmas window display at Eaton's and Simpsons or the Macy's Thanksgiving Day parade.

Marketing to today's consumer market is vastly different than it was fifty and sixty years ago. Back in those days, commercial messaging took the form of what marketers refer to as, the shotgun approach. This is similar to fishing with a large fish net. Rather than the person who fishes for sport who is always trying to snare that big one, fishnet is used by commercial fishers to catch as money fish as possible within its nets. No precision, no sport. It's all about quantity and making the quota.

There was not much advanced technology available to anyone with something to sell in those days. Businesses pretty much had to rely upon newspaper and magazine advertising. Television was a fairly new medium and not every home had a set until the late 1950s. There were also the options of sending catalogues and flyers through the mail or advertising on those large billboards located on or adjacent to buildings and other public structures. That was just about it. And anyone who was interested in advertising their product would do so in any or all of these ways.

As television appeared in more and more homes, advertisers began to put the bulk of their media buys into it. The only visual medium at the time, television advertisers and marketers would spend a great deal of money and time pitching their products to a young and rapidly growing population. Each product had its own distinct identity or personality. There was Ronald Macdonald, Tony the Tiger, Joe Camel, Mr. Clean and the Maytag Repairman, just to name a few. Clever slogans and jingles were developed to stick in the minds of consumers. Who can forget Ho Ho Ho, Green Giant, or Plop, plop, fizz, fizz, oh what a relief it is, and I'd like to teach the world to sing in perfect harmony. All these were used to great effect. Then of course, there was Mr. Whipple telling a trio of women customers in his store: Don't squeeze the Charmins. Or, Trix is for kids, and a great classic, Sorry Charlie, but only the best tasting tuna gets to be Star Kist. All these still resonate with those who lived through this period.

For the most part, these ads spoke to multiple generations simultaneously. Oh sure market segmentation and targeting existed, but it was at best quite crude in its application. Beer and tire commercials would appear during football or hockey telecasts. Dish soap, detergent and baking product ads would be seen during the daytime soaps for all the *stay at home* moms. Toy commercials would air Saturday mornings when most children would be watching their weekly fix of cartoons and kids' programming. This is just about as scientific as it got at the time.

By the early 1960s, the leading edge of the baby boom generation was entering their late teens, their impact was being felt in every aspect of modern culture. They influenced everything from fashion to music, art to automobiles, architecture to travel and everything else. Their numbers were overwhelming. It seemed as if everywhere one looked all that could be seen were young people.

A decade synonymous with sex, drugs and rock and roll. Also, popularly referred to as the hippie era or counter culture. They could typically be identified by their appearance. Long hair for men, tie-dye clothes, bell bottom pants, communal living and spending a lot time just, hangin' out.

Although most young people did not adopt the hippie or communal lifestyle, they did go along with the fashion, attitudes, and culture it promoted. Their dress, music and politics were a departure from their parents' generation. The government and big business, or anyone over 30, could not be trusted. They were referred to as *the man*. Protesting U.S. military involvement in Vietnam, joining the new ecology movement, working for equal rights for women was commonplace. Still others joined up to be freedom riders and fight for civil rights and end to the segregation of African Americans in the southern United States.

From the start, the baby boomers re-defined and changed just about every aspect of society, culture and the economy. The first generation brought up on television. They watched the first televised U.S. Presidential debate between Senator John F. Kennedy and Vice President Richard Nixon in 1960, they saw Neil Armstrong walk on the moon and watched reports from Vietnam on the war. They began the movement to preserve the environment. Ended institutional segregation in the southern United States. Stopped a war in south east Asia. And to top it off, when they organized a music festival in upstate New York in the summer of 1969, where over 500,000 young people turned out for a weekend of peace, love and rock n' roll.

There is certainly no market force more predictable then the baby boom generation. Since they first appeared on the scene at the end of World War Two, the baby boom generation have shaped the cultural, economic and social landscape. Government and business were quick to recognize the radical changes that were occurring in the population distribution. To their credit, they responded with all the gusto they could muster.

Now, seven decades later, government and business must similarly respond to these massive shifts in demography. After the last of the baby boom births came to an end in 1965, the fertility rate plummeted. In the following years, there was little back fill to support the aging baby boom population as it careened towards older ages. As a result, the population pyramid has changed from its triangular configuration in the 1950s and 1960s, into what is morphing now into one that resembles that of a mushroom.

Just as the response by government and business to the baby boom population was fast and earnest throughout the 1950s and 1960s, it must be as well now. There is no question government and business are capable. When they were called upon to answer the call at the outset of the baby boom generation, government and business answered that call. Today, they are being called upon again. Society requires a similar response.

6

The Times, They Are A Changin'

L iving longer healthier lives is a great triumph for humanity. Improved nutrition, sanitation, healthcare, better and more effective medicines, education and less poverty, have been the most compelling reasons for increasing life expectancies. However, as people live longer, society as a whole, faces unprecedented, but by no means, insurmountable challenges.

Certainly the timing of these demographic transformations are well known. No government, anywhere on the planet, can make a legitimate claim that it is surprised or caught off guard by it's arrival. After all, demographics, at the end of the day, is about counting people. In fact, a cursory look at any country's current population pyramid and it is easy enough to discern how many 65 year old people there will be 20, 30 or 50 years from now. All these people have already been born. These demographics have been locked in for decades now. To determine future costs to the government treasury, using current dependency based transfer modelling, costs can be determined with fairly accurate precision.

To determine the future fiscal needs of any society, government merely needs to count up the number of people in the various age cohorts. Once this is accomplished, a long term strategic plan with accompanying individual transfer payment and revenue projections can be ascertained for any country in the developed world and for many in the non developed world also.

Unlike other potential contingencies, such as an economic or financial crisis, armed conflict, international trade wars, terrorism, cyber attacks, severe weather events or extreme climate change, just to name a few, pinpointing a date and time when any of these events could occur, is difficult to determine.

Upon becoming Prime Minister of Great Britain, Harold Macmillan was asked by a reporter what he feared the most. It is said Macmillan replied without hesitation, *Events, my dear boy, events*. No matter the size of the mandate or their popularity, democratically elected governments of all political persuasions, whether in a parliamentary or republican style system, can encounter all kinds of difficulties when attempting legislative change. To counter these anticipated challenges, governments take every precaution to prepare sound legislative proposals, briefing materials and talking points anticipating any counter argument that could be advanced. Simulations are run again and again. Speeches are practiced. Nothing is left to chance.

Similarly, when a business decides to make a large scale product change, they could spend years researching, polling, conducting focus groups, to make sure a new product or the reinventing an old one will be successful. Yet, in spite of performing all their due diligence, there are many examples in recent decades, such as New Coke, the Segway and Betamax, and a host of others, that just failed to catch the eye of the consumer.

Demographics do not leave anything to the imagination. As indicated, it's merely a matter of counting. Yet, in spite of it's certainty and predictability, governments and business have largely ignored demographics. There is no question changing demographics move, at least until recently, at glacial speed. But rather than choosing to ignore what they knew was going to eventually occur, the pace of this change should have been greeted as a gift. In other words, a large period of time to prepare and put the right amount of thought into what they knew would ultimately be facing. This would have reduced potential risk factors and left as little room as possible for error. There are no excuses for any government to be caught flat footed at this point with not at least an outline of a plan for transitioning to an aged society.

What is known about the coming demographic changes, is that the cost to the public treasury will be beyond the resources of any government to pay. Not taking action to confront the challenges posed by the aging population, governments are jeopardizing their very fiscal sustainability.

The fiscal implications of population aging has been known for some time. In a 1998 paper by the Honourable Donald Johnston, Secretary General of the Organisation for Economic Cooperation and Development at that time and a former Canadian cabinet minister in the government of Prime Minister Pierre Elliott Trudeau, warned against such inaction. In *The Challenges of Population Aging: An International Perspective*, he wrote the following:

> *"(Population aging) ... there are reasons to be worried. The full impact of aging is now expected to hit our economies very soon, beginning the next decade in many countries. Still, it is not certain that our policymakers have taken the full measure of its consequences: We are talking here about the sustainability of our future social and economic system. If substantial and sustained action is not undertaken, we may face a major societal crisis".*

With longer life expectancies and diminishing fertility rates, populations are currently older than they have ever been in history. What's more, with each passing minute, they continue to age. In 1950, seven of the most populous countries in the developed world were: the United States, Russia, Germany, France, Italy and Britain. By 2050, the only country to remain in this group will be the United States. More so, there are currently 30 countries where there are more people 65 years and over than people under 16 years. Within two years, there will be 35 countries in this group. By 2050, the number of countries with a greater number of people 65 years and over compared to those under 16 years, will increase to a staggering 82.

Based on known average life expectancies over time, longevity has increased more in the last five decades than over the preceding five thousand years. Throughout human history, populations have never been so old.

What's more, accelerating the pace of population aging is an increase in the number of people 85 years and over. Indeed, the fastest growing age segment in the world today are those people who are 85 years and over. To break it down even further, members of the population who fall within the 85 to 99 year old age segment are projected to increase in number sixfold to 1.3 billion by 2050. Those who are 100 years of age and over are expected to increase to 175 million which is sixteen fold their current number.

Increasing life expectancy represent perhaps humanity's greatest crowning achievement to date. It's proof is everywhere. There are a growing number of countries where one can count more walkers on the street than baby carriages. For those who watch of television, listen to the radio or read newspapers and magazines, there are certainly a big increase in the number of ads for hearing aids, dentures and stair lifts.

There are also the growing number of television programmes focusing on an older demographic such as the current hit, *Grace and Frankie* starring Jane Fonda and Lily Tomlin, 81 and 79 respectively. Unlike the hit show from the 1980s, *The Golden Girls*, whose characters resembled most everyone's grandmother, *Grace and Frankie* share a beach house after their husbands have left them for other women. They have an active dating and love life and sport some of the most fashionable clothing. Similarly, in recent feature films, such as, *The Bookclub*, where aging baby boomers are depicted as vibrant, active and modern smashing the stereotype of what used to pass for old age.

As baby boomers age, they are radically changing the conventional wisdom of how old age is viewed. Just like from the moment they first appeared on the scene in 1946, they are taking the economy in a host of new and exciting directions. The addition of two to three decades to their lifespans is not being just tacked on at the end of life. It is rather being distributed in their most productive, creative and active years. This generation would bristle at the mere thought of them becoming dependent or a burden at 65 years. For many, at this age, they are just gearing up to reinvent themselves for a second or third act.

Baby boomers are the wealthiest, best educated, most adventurous, purposeful generation in history. Each day, large swaths of this generation turn 65. For prior generations, it was time to step out of the workforce. For many baby boomers, however, at 65 years, they are just hitting their stride. Studies have shown that this generation is reluctant to slow down and would rather keep working and contributing to society. Many just want to continue to feel a sense of fulfillment. For others, they need to work because they do not have enough financial resources to slow down or stop working altogether.

As an aggregate, the baby boom generation controls a staggering amount of wealth. In the United States, and is proportionately
comparable in other developed countries, the baby boom generation plus four years of the oldest members of Generation X, control
almost 80% of the country's net worth. They are responsible for
over $7 trillion in economic activity which is projected to double
by 2032. If this generation was an economy, it would rank as the
third largest in the world behind the United States and China.

More than 70% of disposable income in the United States
comes from baby boomers. What's more, this is a generation that
likes to spend. They purchase some $3.3 trillion in consumer goods
annually far more than any other age segment. Out of 123 consumer goods categories, they are the top spenders in 119 of them.
They are the number one spenders in every healthcare category.
They account for 75% of all prescription drug sales. They purchase
more new automobiles and spend more on the cars they buy than
any younger age category.

The grandparent economy, created by the baby boom generation, is responsible for spending over $3.2 billion annually in the
United States. As a group, they control over 50% of the financial
assets in the United States. This segment of the population is one of
the fastest growing. Their spending habits are fairly similar across
developed countries. They purchase homes and cars for their grandchildren. Some are even taking out mortgages on their own homes
in order to do so. They also pay for their grandchildren's education,
trips and other leisure activities.

The baby boom generation is like no other that came before.
They came of age in an era where everything was possible. Born
into a post war economy that was booming. By virtue of their large
numbers, they were responsible for the creation and expansion of
whole industries. Clothing, toys, snack foods and more. When they

aged into their teenage years, they were the first generation to to possess significant purchasing power in their own right. This led to a burgeoning fashion and music industry. Illicit drugs were also in abundance. Taken together, this all led to the creation of what became known as the counter culture.

Culminating in the Woodstock music festival in 1969, the baby boom generation has been the dominant force in the economy, politics, culture, consumer trends and social attitudes for the past six decades. What's more, there is no indication that this will change anytime soon. Certainly, when it comes to talkin' about my generation, if you are a baby boomer, you certainly have a lot left to say.

7

The Incredible Shrinking Nations

R emember the 1957 sci-fi pic, *The Incredible Shrinking Man?* Well, now get set for the remake: The Incredible Shrinking Nations. Except this is not science fiction. It's real.

Rapid population aging and plunging fertility rates are threatening the very existence of some nations. Declining populations of this magnitude are unprecedented in human history outside of a major war, famine or disease. According to the United Nations, populations will decline in 48 countries by 2050. In fact, by 2100, they project that most of these countries will have lost half of their population.

Take the Baltic nation of Latvia, for example. In 2000, Latvia's population was 2.38 million. By 2018, the country's population had dropped over 18% to 1.95 million giving it the dubious moniker as the nation with the fastest population decline. Latvia is a country shrinking before the world's eyes.

Not alone, Latvia's Baltic neighbours also had a sharp fall in population. Lithuania registering a 17.5% drop and Georgia not far behind at a 17.2% decline.

Membership in the EU and the opening up of borders has made it easy for residents of these Baltic countries to find employment and opportunity elsewhere. Although the usual suspects such as low fertility and high mortality are certainly to blame, the region suffers from an additional geopolitical ailment. The threat of invasion by Russia hanging over the heads of the Baltic countries in recent years has led to a great deal of anxiety within these populations. As a result, large numbers of working age have emigrated to other countries within in the European Union in search of economic opportunity. Peaking after Russia's annexation of Crimea in 2015, the threat of invasion has somewhat lessened since that time. Nevertheless, there is a long history of mistrust and suspicion among the residents of the Baltic states towards Russia regarding their intentions.

Even with this easing of tensions, the dye has been cast. The large exodus of those from the working age population has brought about an investment chill. As young, able bodied workers are leaving for greener pastures, it is very difficult to attract the attention of global capital. Without international investment, the prospects get even more dim. This just ends up encouraging even more of the working age population to leave.

These seismic demographic changes are not restricted to the Baltic states. The United Nations has forecast that Albania, Bulgaria, Croatia, Moldova, Hungary and Poland will lose an average of 40% of their population by 2100. Leading this group of nations is Moldova, who will see a 52% drop in their population. In fact, the eastern most member states of the European Union, which currently has a population of slightly over 103 million, is projected to plunge to 64 million people by the end of this century. It's a familiar story the Baltic states know well. Young, highly skilled and educated members of the population are leaving to seek better economic opportunity not just for themselves, but also their children.

The International Monetary Fund reported in 2016 that in the previous 25 years, close to 20 million people left Central, Eastern and Southern Europe. This represents 5% of the regions total population. According to the same report, based on an analysis undertaken by the organization, the loss of this vast amount of skilled labour had resulted in lower productivity growth and undermined the regions competitiveness. If this loss of skilled labour had not taken place, the region's cumulative real GDP growth would have been 7 percentage points higher than it was. This staggering amount demonstrates just how critical an exodus of young skilled workers can be for an economy that is already experiencing the negative effects of an aging population.

Even southeast Europe's largest economy, Romania, is not immune. By 2100, it is projected that the country will experience a 40% drop in their population. But unlike other countries in the region, Romania had benefitted from large amounts of foreign capital investment into manufacturing and high tech. In fact, Romania was emerging as a hub for information technology and outsourcing.

So what went wrong?

Romania is on the leading edge of what every other developed country will soon be facing. Crashing head on into a shortage of skilled workers. A recent report by ManpowerGroup, an international recruiting agency, stated that 80% of Romania's businesses identified finding skilled workers as their biggest challenge. Romania's economy was the victim of it's own success. Problem was is that they simply did not have enough workers with the kinds of skills their businesses needed.

Once a population is depleted of it's critical mass of it's young working age residents, a country is hard pressed to recover. Lets take Portugal, as an example. From 2011 to 2014, Portugal was on the brink of economic collapse. It's budget deficit was a staggering

11% of GDP and it's national debt 130% of GDP. Almost 500,000 people of working age left the country many of whom were highly educated and skilled. In the end, the country required an IMF rescue package which required the government to adhere to a programme of strict austerity.

Five years after it has exited the IMF's bailout programme, Portugal's economy is fairing relatively well. In fact, it has made quite a remarkable recovery. However, in spite of this, it faces a number of challenges that puts long term sustainability in question.

With the exodus of many of it's young and highly educated workers and the time it has taken for a recovery to kick in, Portugal may have passed a tipping point. For the country's economy to make a fully recovery and promise a stable future for its population, it is going to take much more than just fiscal discipline at this point.

Much of Portugal's current economic gains are attributable to the zero interest rate policy of the European Central Bank and a spike in the country's tourism. So, although the deficit is down, Portugal's population is aging at a fairly rapid pace, it's national debt is still increasing. A process accelerated by the exodus of close to 20% of its population during the country's economic crisis a decade ago. Many of these came from the all important working age segment many of whom were highly skilled and educated. All this talent departed for elsewhere. Getting them back after years of living abroad, growing their careers, raising a family and planting roots, will be an extremely difficult task.

With a population that is rapidly aging, Portugal's largest public expenditure is the country's pension system. Current demographic trends show this will increasingly intensify. By 2030, at least 25% of the country's population will be 65 years or over. Recognizing this big hole in its key demographic age segment, Portugal's government knows it needs to either bring back many of those young workers that have left or attract new ones. Either way, they need to beef up their working age pool to provide enough revenue to provide support for its growing pension obligations.

To try to get it's former residents to return, a number of incentives have been offered by the government. A number of proposals have been offered by the government such as a 50% tax reduction for those who left before 2016 and return before 2021. The government is also offering citizenship to anyone who invests at least one million euros or creates 10 jobs. Such measures have been attempted in other European Union countries with very modest results. In the meantime, those who currently reside in Portugal are subject to increasing taxes, user fees and a 23% value added tax.

So while Portugal's economy may have rebounded, it appears, similar to the Baltic states. Once a country loses a significant number of it's working age segment, it just may pass a point of no return. Even with significant policy change, such as replacing the dependency model and expanding it's labour base, Portugal's long term outlook appears to be rather bleak.

The respected medical journal, *The Lancet*, followed population trends in every country from 1950 to 2017. They observed that the global average fertility rate was 4.7 births per woman at the beginning of the study but dropped to 2.4 by it's conclusion. What they further observed was astonishing. Looking at the study country by country, they found that half of the world's countries have fallen below the replacable fertility rate. Some researchers have taken this to mean that with a fertility rate this low the ultimate sustainability of some nations may be in jeopardy. This has large geo-political and global economic implications which are unprecedented.

Japan has served as the poster child for aging populations. It was just a generation ago many concluded that Japan's ascension to economic superpower status was a foregone conclusion. Due to a weak U.S. dollar vis-a-vis Japan's yen, during the 1980s, Japanese companies went on a buying spree in the United States. Nothing seemed too big or too expensive. U.S. corporate icons such as Firestone, Columbia Pictures and the crown jewel of New York real estate, Rockefeller Centre, were snapped up finding themselves in the hands of Japanese ownership by the end of the decade.

Politicians, academics, media and the U.S. public feared that the buying spree would never end. The locus of economic power seemed to be shifting from New York to Tokyo. There was discussion in policy circles that Japan would soon come to be the world's dominant economy supplanting that of the United States. Paul Kennedy's, *The Rise and Fall of the Great Powers*, published in 1987, led the bestseller list and was on just about everyone's nightstand. His theory was that America, like other great powers before them, had their day in the sun and were now being overaken by those coming up behind them just as the U.S. had done themselves many years before. He wrote about America's increasing sovereign debt, military overstretch and growing trade deficits were signs that the economic hegemony of the United States was in decline. Replacing the U.S. would be Asia's ascending powers, Japan and China.

But by the early 1990s, the wheels came off Japan's economy. Inflation increased, Bank of Japan began raising rates and the stock market plummeted. The U.S. dollar gained strength and the yen lost it. Three decades later, Japan's economy, although the world's third largest, poses no threat to America's status as the world's biggest economy. The U.S. is still the dominant economic power in the world and is showing no signs of relinquishing that title anytime soon.

The United States, unlike any other country on earth, has one major advantage. Sure it has an aging population, but it will not become aged for some time yet. According to the United Nations, the United States has the highest projected population growth of any developed country with an expected increase of 21% by 2050. People from around the world yearn to come to America. It's immigration rate remains high. Illegal immigration is also a significant factor. Although no one knows the precise number, estimates are that undocumented aliens in the United States may be as high as 10 million. Most entered the United States as young adults and are part of the important working age demographic. The majority of them fall into the unskilled category, but America has a shortage of workers of all kinds.

In addition, U.S. Customs and Border Protection has processed over 300,000 claims for refugee status at the U.S. - Mexico border for the first four months of 2019 alone. Once processed, the applicants are required to appear before a judge for a determination hearing to find out if they qualify to remain in the United States as refugees. No other country on earth have people lined up in the tens of thousands on a daily basis wanting to enter a country other than the United States. So, even with a fetility rate is below replacement, America's population continues to grow. No other country has this kind of advantage. As a result, America will avoid many of the demographic pressures gripping just about every other country around the world.

The late Hans Rosling, a noted Swedish demographer, believed that countries with high fertility rates had promising economic futures. However, it has to be a stretch to believe that countries such as Afghanistan, Niger and Uganda, although boasting high fertility rates from just under four to as high as seven, could possibly hold much promise as future store houses of economic power. In fact, countries with rates of high fertility, without accompanying economic opportunity, could potentially serve as breeding grounds for political instability.

Then there is China. The most populous country in the world, second largest economy behind the United States. It has set astounding rates of economic growth in recent years and it continues to surge. With GDP growth averaging 10% a year over the past four decades, many believed it would soon supplant the United States as the world's economic superpower.

However, it appears that the days of China clocking in at 8% and 9% rates of growth are coming to an end. The International Monetary Fund has revised China's outlook for the coming decade to be between a 5% and 6% rate of growth. There are other even projecting a growth rate of as little as 2%. A far cry from recent years. Acknowledging this demographic change, China's Premier Li Keqiang said on March 5, 2019, at the annual National People's Congress meeting, *We must be fully prepared for a tough struggle.*

The economic challenges China is currently facing are 40 years in the making. It's the old addage, the chickens are now coming home to roost scenario.

In 1979, in an effort to control the growth of its population, China's central government implemented what is infamously known as the *One Child Policy*. China's leaders were concerned about the rapid growth of the country's population since the 1949 revolution. They feared the country would lack the necessary resources to support such a large population.

China's fertility rate in 1960 was 6.0 per woman. As a result of four decades of the one child policy, China's fertility rate is now at 1.5 births per woman. Needless to say, it was certainly successful in achieving its objective. Perhaps even too effective.

China's rise to economic superstardom was a result of both their decision to move toward toward a greater market based economy and a very large working age population. The country appeared to have an inexhaustible supply of young labour. This kept labour costs down leading to cost competitive exports and large levels of foreign investment. However, by limiting the number of births, years later, China no longer has anywhere near the number of people in the working age population it once had. What was once their ace in the hole, is no longer.

By 2027, according to the Chinese Academy of Social Sciences, it is projected that China's population will enter a period of negative growth. The population is expected to decrease by 2.5% or 28 million people by 2050. This will have the effect, according to IMF projections, of causing a labour shortage in China beginning between 2020 and 2025.

In an effort to increase births, the *One Child Policy* was changed to a *Two Child Policy* in 2016. But it has not worked. In 2016, there were 17.9 million births, in 2017 there were 17.2 million and in 2018 the number of births fell once again to 15.2 million. Those who are 65 years of age and over will grow 60% by 2020 and its working age population will decrease by 35% in the same time period.

In the end, China did achieve its goal of population reduction. But it is paying a heavy price for it. China now has a rapidly diminishing population, massive reduction in the number of working age and a rapidly aging population. There are also 70 million more young men than young women in China. During the years of the *One Child Policy,* since boys are valued more than girls in Chinese culture, many girls were aborted. This now raises the issue as to where all these young men will find brides for themselves.

In 2010, China's 65 year and over population was 8% of it's population. By 2050, it will be 24%. According to the Peking Union Medical College, the proportion of the country's total expenditure on pensions, medical care, senior care, and welfare will increase from it's current level of 7.3% to 26.2% of GDP by 2050. These expenditures will put tremendous fiscal pressures on the central government. Because China's economy is so intricately linked to most other countries around the world, the economic implications will ripple through the global economy like falling dominoes.

Below replacement value fertility rates are the most significant factor behind de-population. In some countries, the fertility rate has fallen so low that the number of deaths have exceeded the number of births each year.

Further accelerating declining populations, is migration. Large movements of people from one country or region to another. These movements are even occuring within countries. In fact, since 2017, there are now more people living in urban centres than rural areas than ever before in history.

The migration from rural to urban communities has profound implications. It is typically the young who depart seeking greater economic opportunity. This leads to a hollowing out of a country's rural areas. The net result of the migration has left many of these communities with populations that skew much older than the general population. As a result, local services suffer due to a smaller tax base. The political influence of areas with lower population also results in diminishing significance at the governing table where important decisions are made.

The exodus of young people from rural areas has resulted in these regions aging faster than the country's national average. For older residents of rural communities, they face greater challenges than their counterparts in urban centres. Access to adequate health services are the most significant challenge. For instance, the biggest and the best hospitals are located in the larger urban centres. In order to access these facilities, aged rural residents will be forced to travel long distances in order to receive the care they require.

Diminishing populations in rural areas are also leading to a reduction in transportation services. Fewer residents mean fewer travellers. Transportation companies in rural regions have therefore cut service on unprofitable routes. This has made getting from point A to point B a real challenge for many elderly people in rural areas. The real problem arises when there is a need for an elderly person to get to a large urban centre for specialized healthcare services or treatment. In many instances, there is no direct service. As a result, aged residents of these communities are forced to travel as much as a day to access the healthcare services they require.

Rural communities are seeing increased levels of poverty as a result of the exodus of the young. Women are particularly hard hit. Making lower wages then men throughout their working lives, more time given to caregiving and a longer life expectancy, have made them especially vulnerable. The gender gap continues when old age benefits are recieved. Women, who earned less when employed, will find they receive less in benefit payments than a male thus perpetuating the gender gap even when it comes to old age benefits. This has resulted in what demographers refer to as the *feminization of aging.*

As countries continue to age and urbanize, many of the rural areas that at one time served as regional hubs, may dwindle in size to the point where they cease to exist altogether. Governments must therefore develop plans for population aging in rural areas which will be quite different from the urban agenda. Indeed, urban centres need to take notice of the current blight of rural areas. Much of what is occuring currently in these areas is what is in store for urban centres in the absence of effective policy reform.

Migration, whether its internal or external, could have serious political, social and economic implications for a country. When there is a large movement over time of a working age population from one part of a country to another, deep economic cleavages can develop. Areas experiencing economic prosperity may find there are growing feelings of animus directed at their poorer regional cousins. This would particularly be acute if they are required to subsidize them through what is perceived to be an unfair formula of equalization payments.

When the country as a whole loses population through migration, this could lead to serious geopolitical consequences. A lower population could seriously diminish a country's political or economic influence in global affairs. Such a country, in an effort to maintain it's self percieved stature, may become more belligerent or reckless on the world stage upsetting relations with its neighbours, the region or globally.

It could also lead to an increase in tensions or strained relations between countries. This recently occurred between the United States and Mexico. The U.S. President criticized the Mexican government for allowing caravans of migrants to enter Mexico through it's southern border. Relations between the two countries became especially tense when President Trump threatened to shut down America's southern border altogether if Mexico's government did not take more effective action to reduce the number of migrants allowed to enter their country.

This issue has also caused intense partisan debate in the United States. Perhaps currently the biggest issue in the country, which has its origins in the barrios of Central and South America. Not only has this crisis highlighted an urgency for immigration reform, it has impacted America's foreign policy relationships in the region and around the world. Some argue if America provided increased economic aid for countries in Central America, there would be greater economic opportunity negating the reason for them to want to leave in the first place.

Needless to say, population aging and shifting demographics through the movement of large numbers of people, have profound implications that go far beyond fiscal matters. The change in demography of just a single country can upset geopolitical balances resulting in an alteration in international relationships and regional orders.

In a highly globalized world, nothing is local any longer. Every country, region and continent are seemingly tied at the hip. What may appear to be an insignificant occurrence in some remote global location, could have profound international implications.

Demographics are the key. They cannot be ignored. Country after country has done so at their own peril. For most countries it is not too late to act. Positive outcomes are still achievable. But they will not be for long. For those countries who have time to act, the opportunity to do so is limited. It is imperative they undertake significant policy change immediately so their own transition to an aged society is seamless and equitable for the country's entire population regardless of age.

8

Plausible Deniability?

In today's hyper partisan, contrarian and highly opinionated world, it is rare to achieve agreement on just about anything. It is more common today for a person to have their *truth* and another to have their own. Each believing their truth is the valid one. But how can both be truth? Well, they cannot. For instance, $1 + 1 = 2$. It cannot ever equal three.

As Aristotle would say, *The high minded man must care more for the truth than for what people think*. Separating truth from thought, he would have people believe that the two are separate and distinct. The latter being subjective or interpretive. Opinions, in other words. Whereas, the former is the absolute. So rare is an absolute devoid of opinion that when such occurs it is to be trumpeted for all to hear. Such is the case of population aging.

Slow, methodical and plodding are adjectives one can use to describe changes in demography. It is for this reason they serve as an early warning system for the need to recalibrate public policy to prepare for any changes the new population distribution will bring. Decades in the making, even longer as in the case of France, which first started to age over one hundred years ago, societies have had ample time to prepare. Even more so when the change in demographic structure is facilitated by way of social engineering. China's *One-Child Policy* is the best example of this where parents were restricted to having one child in an effort to slow down the country's population growth. It's outcome should have been planned for with an ability to respond effectively.

Unlike waking up to a surprise snowstorm when not so much as a flurry could be seen in the air the night before, there is a determinism to demography. Demographic projections are based on the population's own past. In other words, if someone is twenty-nine years of age this year, they will be thirty years of age one year later. Such is demographic forecasting.

However, notwithstanding any specific country's own demography, there is not a government in the world currently prepared to effectively respond to their own shifting population structures.

With all the evidence hiding in plain sight, why have governments been neglecting the most profound change ever to occur in the modern world? Well, let's take a look at why governments have been reluctant to act.

When the baby boom generation came of age beginning in the mid 1960s, the developed world began to enter a demographic sweet spot. Unprecedented growth in the working age population matched with what appeared to be an insatiable desire to consume. There seemed to be no end to the numbers of young people entering the work force. As the working age population increased so to did the dependency ratio. Governments had more money from tax revenues than they knew what to do with. Massive spending on healthcare, education, poverty, and social programmes were launched which made up what was known in the United States as the Great Society. This is what is referred to as a *demographic dividend*.

Then in the late 1980's, China's working age population of 700 million were brought on stream. This development doubled the world's working age population. This put China's economy on a fast track to stellar economic performance. Not only was labour plentiful, but it was also cheap by western standards. As a result, large multinationals began to re-locate their manufacturing facilities to China to save on labour costs. But, while this was occuring, something else was afoot which would ultimately lead to a souring of the sweet spot.

As China's economy was growing, fertility rates around the world were dropping. The working age population declined and so did dependency ratios. Decreasing and rapidly aging populations have resulted in the proverbial double whammy which have impacted financial stability, productivity growth and fiscal sustainability.

As populations age and diminish in size, there will be a negative impact economic growth. For those experiencing low growth and high debt, their future appears bleak. Similarly, as people live longer, healthier lives than ever before, they will need additional resources. Anticipating to live to a certain age then going well beyond it requires more savings that was not planned for during the years they were working. If they feel compelled to liquidate their stock market portfolios, it could trigger financial instability. Further undermining economic stability is an increase in age related spending. This will grow from from 16% to 25% of GDP by 2100.

Although the population has been aging for decades, due to it's slow progression, it feels as if it does not have a sense of serious urgency. Let's take a look at the development of population aging as an issue. Maybe it has simply not been part of the discussions or deliberations when nations assemble to discuss the salient issues impacting the world.

Population aging has been on the global agenda for over 70 years. It made it's first appearance in 1948, when the delegation from Argentina to the United Nations presented a Draft Resolution on a *Declaration of Old Age Rights* to the General Assembly. The resolution declared:

> *Old age rights, having the same origin and purpose as other universal social safeguards … .*

It goes on to create rights to *assistance, accommodation, food, clothing, care of physical health, care of moral health, recreation, work, stability and respect as necessary for safeguarding.* It was under serious consideration by UN member states to establish a declaration for the protection of old age rights. In the end, it was rejected. However, instead of it's own stand alone declaration, a more broad reference to security in old age was included in Article 25 of the Universal of Declaration of Human Rights.

Over the next three decades, there was little discussion on age. What discussions there was focused on over population. But by the late 1970s, the subject began to pick up a significant head of steam. As fertility rates were dropping and life expectancy was increasing, the IMF began to express concern. After all, as the back stop against countries that got themselves into severe fiscal crises, it would be the IMF that would be required to bail them out.

Once the IMF became earnestly involved in the discussions on population aging, countries took notice before they would be put on notice. The UN General Assembly decided to convene a World Assembly on Aging to take place in 1982. The purpose of the World Assembly was to provide a forum to *launch an international action programme aimed at guaranteeing economic and social security to older persons, as well as opportunities to contribute to national development.* The General Assembly further indicated that the World

Assembly *should result in societies responding more fully to the social-economic implications of the aging of populations to the specific needs of older persons.*

The World Assembly subsequently issued the Vienna International Plan of Action. Essentially re-affirming the rights contained in the 1948 Universal Declaration on Human Rights, but also called on the world to pay attention to the *serious problem besetting a growing portion (older) populations of the world.*

To mark the 10th anniversary of the Vienna International Plan of Action, the United Nations decided to declare that 1999 would be observed as the International Year of Older Persons. However, it was not until 2002, that the landmark Madrid International Plan of Action on Ageing (MIPAA) was adopted by the Second World Assembly on Ageing. The MIPAA remains to this day as the leading international instrument on the subject.

MIPAA is the first internationally agreed upon document that addresses the fundamental challenge posed to countries to *build a society for all ages.* Focusing on three areas, the MIPPA offers a bold agenda.

- *Older persons and development*
- *Advancing health and well-being into old age*
- *Ensuring enabling and supportive environments*

Serving as a political declaration, the MIPAA suggests ways for governments, businesses and other organizations to establish how their own societies can best interact and care for their aging population. Although agreed to by 159 countries, MIPAA is a voluntary instrument. Adherence to the agreement relies on the amount which each country is prepared to make by way of policy change and budgetary commitment.

All this information is widely known by governments the world over. Non-governmental organizations such as the United Nations, Organisation for Economic Cooperation and Development, the World Health Organization, the International Monetary Fund and the World Bank, have all made it clear that the speed at which the population is aging and how it requires immediate attention. It's not even as if government at all levels around the world are not aware of the issue. They have all recognized it themselves as a critical issue that will affect pensions, healthcare, work, fiscal policy, productivity and innovation. Yet, governments are still reluctant to act.

Perhaps its worth taking a look at those times when government has taken action. Maybe that will yield some clues. Let's take a look.

In 1995, Italian Prime Minister, Silvio Berlusconi's government withstood one political crisis after another. Yet, when it came to the issue of pension reform, his coalition shattered. At the same time, the government of Holland repealed legislation it had just enacted to cut retirement benefits. They retreated after the sudden rise in popularity of the Pension Party was threatening their own hold on power. Similar parties sprung up in other countries, such as, Israel. The one common link between all these parties was that they had significant support from their countries older voters. In all instances, there was sufficient enough opposition to the government's proposal that they all back tracked.

Eight years after their first attempt, the government of Italy once again tried to reform retirement pensions. Faced with it's pensions making up 15% of it's GDP, one of the hightest in Europe at the time, external pressure from other European Union countries to act was intense. Yet, when the government proposed changes, 5.5 million people took to the streets in protest.

Similarly, when the government of France decided to change the country's official retirement age from 60 to 62 in 2010, millions took to the streets to protest the proposal.

In 2018, the governments of Belguim, Coatia and Russia, all proposed changes to their retirement regimes. In all three countries, there were massive protests against the move.

In 2012, the government of Canada, under the Conservative Party, proposed increasing the country's retirement age from 65 to 67. Organized labour, seniors' organizations and the opposition parties in Canada's Parliament all opposed the move. In the 2015 election, the Liberal Party was victorious winning a majority of seats in the country's Parliament in part because they had promised to restore the retirement age to 65.

Canada even had an earlier experience with an effort to reduce Old Age Security payments. In 1985, the Conservative government that had been elected the year before with the largest majority in Canadian electoral history, proposed de-indexing Old Age Security payments. Objections were fast and furious. The proposal was soon abandoned.

There is no doubt governments are aware of the challenges posed by the aging population. However, it seems as if populations in general are not aware of the need to act. When governments do take action, they are either defeated at the polls in the next election or they withdraw their proposals in the face of large protests by their own populations.

Compare this to those countries where governments have been successful in taking action. Some countries that have taken the bold step of increasing the official retirement age are the United Kingdom, United States, and Australia. Needless to say, these were not popular moves when they were undertaken. Yet, these governments succeeded in doing so.

People certainly do not want to believe that a system of entitlements and social programmes that have worked for so long and
served their own parents well, will not at least do as well for themselves and their own children. Populations do not necessarily have
to agree with the move, but they must understand the need for it in
order for it to be successful. Reform of public pension has been the
subject of discussion in these countries for many years leading up
to the change in policy.

The longer governments wait to act, the more difficult it will
be. Although countries are aging at differing paces, it is imperative
that all begin to immediately engage their populations in a dia-
logue on this important issue. Populations need to be educated and
understand that increased longevity may require some personal
sacrifice.

Kicking the aging can down the road is no longer an option.
Governments must take on the challenges posed by population aging immediately. The situation grows more dire by the day. The
facts are clear. All the evidence is in and it is ironclad. There is
certainly no case to be made for any kind of plausible deniability.

9

What Do Pensions And 2008 Have In Common?

If I were re-locating into some stage that had a huge unfounded pension plan, I'm walking into liabilities. "I say to myself, Why do I wanna build a plant there that has to sit there for 30 or 40 years? Because I'll be here for the life of the pension plan and they'll come after corporations, they'll come after individuals. They just - they're gonna have to raise a lotta money.

Warren Buffett, CNBC - March 2, 2019

P hew, the world really dodged a bullet. The 2008 global financial crisis was the worst economic downturn since the Great Depression. The global economy was pushed to the precipice. At the time, it looked for a moment as if the world's financial system was about to go over the edge. Like the cavalry coming across the hill at the last moment to rescue the beleaguered troops, the arrival of governments to re-capitalize markets came just in the nick of time. Trillions of dollars were ultimately sunk by governments into troubled banks in an effort to save them from collapse. Had this not occurred, the global economy could have very well been lost. In the words of former U.S. President George W. Bush, *This sucker could go down.*

The 2008 global financial crisis rocked the world economy to its very core. It came within a hair's width of a complete collapse. In an effort to put some fuel into the economic engines, the G20 governments agreed to inject a stimulus equal to 4% of GDP into their respective economies. Central banks did their part on the monetary side by slashing interest rates to provide cheap money to business for expansion and job creation.

During the recession that ensued, government budget deficits soared. Declining revenue, massive injections of government money into the economy and increased social payments, all added to existing national debt. Global economic developments triggered a worldwide banking crisis and credit crunch. As a result, borrowing costs increased and financing all but dried up.

Greece emerged as the first country unable to service its mounting debt. Borrowing costs spiked and credit rating agencies downgraded the country's sovereign debt to junk status. There was concern that the country would even default on it's debt. Other countries soon followed. Portugal, Italy, Ireland and Spain all required massive bail outs from the other European Union governments and the International Monetary Fund.

Efforts to reduce budget deficits by raising taxes and cutting expenditures did little to restore confidence. Rather, it resulted in social unrest as large numbers of people took to the streets in protest. The global economy was teetering on a razor's edge.

However, a decade after the crisis began, global markets have been on a prolonged bull run now for almost as long with no end in sight. In spite of ongoing strong economic reports, the financial crisis starkly exposed the fragility of the global economy. It showed how globalization has inextricably linked capital markets and the fiscal fate of countries.

Finanical sector support and government bailouts cushioned the global economy from the worst of the crisis. However, in the period following, the national debt of countries has increased to unprecedented levels. The rapid aging of the population has exposed governments to future contingent liabilities that will pose severe fiscal challenges further adding to mounting levels of national debt.

But unlike what occured during the 2008 global financial crisis when the cavalry came charging over the hill to rescue the soon to be ambushed troops at the bottom, the next battle will require more than a mere cavalry to rescue it. Pension promises strained by aging populations and increasing retirements have the potential to pose a crisis that will make 2008 look like amateur hour.

There was a time when people would take leave from the workfore to embark on their retirement years could expect to live approximately a decade. However, as life expectancy increases, those who take retirement at their country's qualifying age, can now expect to live two or three decades more. Living for a decade on savings and pension plans typically kept retirees comfortable. But living twenty or thirty years longer, although a great triumph of humanity, will put a significant strain on pension systems stretching them to the breaking point.

As far as state pensions go, as the number of people aged 65 years and over increase, the number of young workers replacing them are decreasing. With fertility rates in developed countries below the replacement value of 2.1, the outlook does not show any indications this will change anytime soon.

Today's pension systems were not designed for current life expectancies. For the six countries with the largest public pension systems, Australia, Canada, Japan, Netherlands, the United

Kingdom and the United States, life expectancy is eight to eleven years longer than they were designed for. This means governments are faced with paying out benefits for two to three times longer than anticipated.

As a result of a declining pool of younger workers and an increasing number of those 65 years and over, governments will find themselves under increasing fiscal pressure to meet their obligations to fund old age pensions. However, because systems differ from country to country and as each country's population ages at a different pace, some are more fiscally vulnerable to these pressures than others.

In the United States, for instance, the Social Security system, first proposed by President Franklin Roosevelt in 1936,was establsihed to help older Americans cope during the economic carnage of the great depression. The plan was to fund the system based on what is referred to as, *pay as you go*. In other words, today's workers would pay into a trust fund to pay for their own retirement once that time had come. Following the threshold set in Germany, the United States set their age of eligibility at 65 years.

The Social Security Trust Fund is America's retirement fund. It serves as an intergenerational compact where workers from one generation supported their predecessors. The concept is based on a redistributive principle. Workers, who are assumed to be more well off than retirees, are expected to support them so they are not forced into poverty. The current set of workers would in turn expect to be supported by workers who followed them when they left the workforce. This is the derivation of the principle of *entitlements*.

Currently, 90% of U.S. workers pay into Social Security. In turn, some 68 million receive a Social Security benefit. A total of 68 million Americans receive a Social Security benefit and 90% of workers pay into the trust fund. Although the U.S. population is aging, it is doing so slower than any other OECD member country. Current actuarial projections are that annual revenues from the dedicated payroll tax and taxation of Social Security benefits will be sufficient to fund at least 74% of the anticipated benefits through 2090.

Based on a GDP growth rate of 1.98% and an unemployment rate of 4.5%, the Social Security Trust will never run a deficit. However, with the U.S. economy currently coming in with GDP growth of 3% and unemployment at 3.8%, the country is sitting in the cat bird seat.

Other countries, however, are not as fortunate. The shifting demographic structures are taking many down a path which will leave future generations a legacy liability that will need to be paid by future generations. By way of simple extrapolation from the current population distribution, tax revenues and anticipated age related expenditures clearly demonstrate that public pensions will simply come up short. The fiscal shortfall will determine just how much taxes will need to be increased and/or programme benefits need to be reduced to maintain the sustainability of public pensions in the future.

A country great concern on this score, is China. In Beijing at the Chinese People's Consultative Conference in early 2019, the country's leaders indicated that social security pensions and the aging population as one of their five priorities for the upcoming year. The agreed that what was needed was to *improve the basic pension for retirees and a base pension for urban and rural residents.*

In a culture that has traditionally placed a high premium on respect for the elderly, if the government does not provide an adequate social security pension to age with dignity, it will be viewed as an afront to the people of China. The government bares even a greater responsibility to take care of the aged than they otherwise would because it is they who restricted families to one child. Had this restriction not been imposed, there would be greater numbers of children and grandchildren to care for their own aging family.

Collection of the funds needed for the administration of China's pension system is done so on a local basis. Due to its lack of central control, the process is characterized by gross inefficiencies due to bureaucratic inertia, local deal making and fragmentation. The process for collection was centralized with a January 1, 2019, implementation date, but it has been a challenge getting local authoriites to completely cooperate. Also, as employer contributions are high, there are many who do not pay or they will fudge actual employee numbers in order to reduce the real amount owing to the government. This has resulted in many employees either receiving reduced pension benefits or no payments at all.

According to a recent report by the China Academy of Social Sciences, six provinces declared operating shortfalls when it came to monies collected for pension payments. This is projected to increase to 50% of the provinces coming up short by 2022.

At an average of 9%, China has been at the forefront of economic growth for for over a decade now. However, jeopardizing China's rapid economic growth and the reason it will not overtake the U.S. economy, is simply because it has run out of runway. It ran out of what put them in the hunt in the first place. It's overwhelming number of working age people.

China has reached a demographic tipping point. A legacy of the one-child policy, by 2050, one-third of China's population will be 60 years and over. The country's dependency ratio will fall from its current level of 3.1 to one, to an alarming 1.3 to one by 2050. Current pensions deficits will increase leading to the need for additional government subsidies. But with a weakening economy, diminishing GDP, a not so favourable trade deal in the offing with the United States, China's economy is in for a very rough ride.

In Canada, there there are currently 5.8 million recipients of old age security receiving a total of $52.2 billion. Due to the fact that Canada is one of the most rapidly aging countries in the OECD and the fastest aging in the Western Hemisphere, by 2030, the number of those receiving benefits will spike to 9.3 million. This will increase total payments to levels upwards of $109 billion. By 2060, when 27% of Canada's population will be 65 years of age and over, the projected cost of Old Age Security payments will be a staggering $246.5 billion. This is in sharp contrast to 2010, when total Old Age Security payments were $36 billion.

Old Age Security payroll deductions in Canada when received by government are placed in general revenues. This is unlike Social Security deductions in the United States where paycheque deductions go directly into a segregated trust fund. The Canada Pension Plan and Quebec Pension Plan are somewhat similar in nature to the Social Security Trust Fund in so far as they are paid from an investment fund that is administered by an independent but public agency. Any reform to Canada's Old Age Security system, because it is a social programme and not an entitlement, will need to be part of an overall change to fiscal policy itself.

Canada's rapidly diminishing dependency ratio will not only jeopardize the future of Old Age Security, but will also touch on additional transfers such as healthcare and other age related expenditures. All what many refer to as the third rail of Canadian society. This makes the ensuing political debate in Canada far more complicated. Many will see having such a discussion as the thin edge of the wedge leading to the dismantling of the country's single payer healthcare system.

Apart from state run old age security pensions, there are a galaxy of additional public pensions that are distinct from the former. These are the pension schemes that are under federal, provincial, state and municipal jurisdiction. Civil servants, teachers and public safety agencies, just to mention a few, administer their own pension schemes. Although Canada's pensions are in pretty good overall shape, south of the border is a different story. Many are like watching a train wreck in slow motion.

In 2016, Citibank reported on the state of public pensions in 20 of the largest countries in the OECD. What they concluded, please sit down for this, no really, sit down, there is a collective shortfall of $78 trillion in these plans. What's more, by 2050, the gap is expected to grow to $400 trillion.

To put this into perspective, if the $78 trillion in pension gap was a country, it would be the largest in the world. Larger than the combined economies of the United States, China, Japan, Germany and the United Kingdom and the next fifteen after that, combined. It's an absolute behemoth.

In Britain, for example, the 350 largest companies in the UK have assets of $950 billion. But, there pension payment obligations are at $1.15 trillion. The country's Pension Protection Fund, which was created to bail out any of the UK's pensions in the event of a collapse, have said that of the 5,945 pensions, just 16% are in surplus. In the U.S., the public pension deficit, including listed companies, is over $4 trillion. France is facing a similar situation. Its pension fund liabilities are 350% of its GDP. The UK and Germany are 320% of GDP.

There are a number of factors contributing to this situation not least of which is population aging and increasing average life expectancies. However, there are additional factors that are also contributing to this situation.

For the better part of the last decade, central banks have engage in a practice called, quantitative easing. A monetary policy tool, it occurs when a country's central bank buys up government or its member's securities in order to keep interest rates low and thereby increase the supply of money. Since the end of the 2008 recession, central banks used this strategy resulting in a flat lining of interest rates. Whereas most pensions have traditionally assumed an annual return of 6%, as a result of quantitative easing, returns have come in at 3%, at best. All this as pensions were paying out more than they were taking in.

Defined benefit (DB) plans, is a pension whereby the beneficiary would get paid a fixed amount, usually 75% of final salary, at the time of retirement. Under a DB plan, the company is required to set aside money to cover future pension obligations. If there investments did not provide enough money to cover benefits when the time came, it was up to the company to make up any shortfall. As beneficiaries live longer, the DBs must be prepared to pay out for longer than they had anticipated.

The demographic dilemma facing DBs is exacerbated by low bond yields. The income from government and fixed income bonds have always served as a cornerstone for pension revenue. From a high of 16% in 1980, bond yields have fallen. Current yields in the United States for 10-Year Treasury is 2.75%, Canada 10 Year Bond is 1.86% and the UK 10 Year Gilt comes in at 1.3%. So with pension investment returns averaging 3%, an employee would need to save 15% each year in order to achieve a pension payout equal to 75% of their final salary. Before quantitative easing, when yields averaged 6% annual return, a worker could achieve 75% of final pay as pension income by saving 8% of their salary over a four decade long working life.

On top of the paltry yield on bonds, DB investments in equities took a beating during the 2008 financial crisis. Although many of those losses have been recovered over the course of the current decade long bull market, the strong market have made additional stock purchases expensive. However, although assets within many of these plans have increased, liabilities to its members have increased more significantly resulting in large and growing pension deficits.

One can clearly see why DB plans are not a scheme of choice for employers. Not only do they have to assume all the risk for making investment decisions, they are required by government to make up any difference in the event of a shortfall. Legislation also requires companies to maintain a certain level of solvency, thereby keeping money on hand they could otherwise use for re-investment.

For this reason, companies have been converting their DB plans over the years to Defined Contribution Plans (DC). Under these schemes, companies have a no-cost way to de-risk from their DB pension obligations by shifting the investment onus to the employee. This removes any possible funding crisis away from employers by shifting it directly onto to the shoulders of the pensions savers themselves.

Although the number of defined benefit plans have been diminishing over recent years, they still account for more than half of the retirement funds in the developed world. But, as DBs rely on bond yields to fund annual payouts, the low interest rate environment of the last decade combined with flat yield curves has caused them to spend more to get the same annual return. This has resulted in increasing liabilities for pensions.

Low bond yields and expensive share values have presented a significant challenge no matter the plan. With individuals responsible for their own plans, it is virtually a certainty if losses are large enough and affected a large number of people, governments would feel the political heat and decide to assume the liability and cover the payments. After all, they were johnny on the spot when it came time to rescue Wall Street and failing banks when they needed help in 2008. The precedent has been established.

At a time of growing political populism, it would be hard to fathom any government not coming to the rescue of a DC plan that was unable to meet its payment obligations. Any government that had one rule for financial institutions and another for workers would certainly find themselves out of office come the next election.

As noted, DBs are required to maintain a minimum level of solvency liquidity in their plans. There have been attempts to lower the threshold due to the growing difficulty in maintaining these minimum levels due to increasing liability. Others have attempted to persuade workers to accept lower benefits then what they have been promised. Naturally, this comes with a cost. *Pay me now, or pay me later.* To fill the gap, the money must come from somewhere. So investments that could have been used for expansion, research or new product development, must be tapped.

Studies have shown that private pensions are in no better position than their public sector counterparts. For instance, in the U.S., private pensions have a mere 18% of the funds necessary to meet their liabilities. They face a pension gap of $3 trillion. Private plans in the UK fare no better. Their overall level of funding is similarly comes up short at 33%. Pension deficits facing the Standard &Poor's 1500, are $638 billion.

Rapidly shifting demographics mean that pension funds must be prepared to pay out longer. A prolonged low interest rate environment has meant that assets have not grown to keep up with increasing liabilities. The math that gave birth to the industry in the first place is disintegrating. As pension gaps widen, there are serious concerns about the long term viability of the global pension industry.

Pension schemes were established to fund beneficiaries in retirement for ten to fifteen years. As long as most people lived into their seventies, plan administrators were not concerned about their ability to pay out. However, with average life expectancies increasing and many retiring before the official age, there is grave concern as to whether these plans will be able to meet their obligations. Credit rating agencies are concerned over growing funding gaps. To plug these holes in public plans, cities and states are injecting large sums of money. Becoming an increasing share of their own budgets, less money is available for important services such as education, healthcare and infrastructure.

In order to increase returns, some pensions are treading into territory where they are making riskier investment choices in order to increase returns. This makes them vulnerable to a downturn in the economy.

One possible way to avert a pension crisis would be to subject them to a stress test. Similar to the kind of test financial institutions must perform in order to make sure they can absorb losses and pay benefits without requiring a government bailout.

As things stand now, taxpayers are on the hook for a system collapse. Governments may be unwilling to act because they believe they will simply socialize any loss. However, public attitudes have fundamentally changed since the 2008 bailout. The rise of populism, Brexit and the elections of Donald Trump in the United States and Jair Bolsonaro in Brazil as presidents of their respective countries, speak to this change.

Whereas in 2008, many may have been fully prepared to accept their government's use of taxpayer money to bail out Wall

Street, it is doubtful it would be acceptable in the current enviornment. Any collapse of the global pension system would be met with great social unrest and economic instability. It is unlikely populations would be prepared to be on the hook for bailing out pension plans.

In the words of former New York Yankeee all-star catcher, Yogi Berra, *It's deja vu all over again.*

10

The Coming Healthcare Crisis Will Make Everyone Sick

Healthcare systems around the world are on the verge of collapse. Regardless of the country in question, healthcare is taking up a larger share of government's annual budget. With life expectancy continuing to increase, continued success in eliminating communicable diseases and a rise in the incidents of non-communicable diseases, healthcare costs are spiraling out of control. To meet this challenge, governments will need to undertake large scale reform of current healthcare systems.

When the population distribution skewed younger, a hospital centred approach to healthcare made sense. The emergency room treated what were actual emergencies. However, as the population ages, many are relying on the hospital emergency room for managing and treating the growing incidents of chronic illness. They are ill-equipped to deal with long term fluctuating needs of chronic illnesses. Geared towards acute edpisodic care, current settings present a serious challenge. Emergency room treatment is not only the most inefficient, it is the most costly to the system and does nothing to improve quality of care. Rather, it actually detracts from it by having to shift resources from elsewhere in the system and applied to the emergency room.

For healthcare systems to be sustainable, costs need to be reduced. However, the traditional method of cost cutting just won't do any longer. Sure governments can reduce the size of the healthcare budget. They can even do so to the point where they decide not to provide any support whatsoever. That would surely save money, but it's not realistic. Neither, however, is a system that is designed to grow revenue based on the number of procedures performed built upon a foundation of fee for service. This is hardly a prescription to reduce cost curves. Quite the contrary.

As populations rapidly age, healthcare systems need to adapt to ensure that people with greater lifespan also benefit from an increased healthspan. Let's face it, anyone given the opportunity to live an extra ten, twenty or thirty years would not want to spend that time confined to a hospital bed or suffering from all sorts of major illnesses. Naturally, they would want to spend these years in good health. To achieve this outcome, healthcare needs to focus more on wellness rather than illness. A sustainable healthcare regime will integrate the social determinants of health such as, education, housing and employment and apply technology to achieve a continuum of care focused on each individual's lifespan.

Healthcare can no longer afford to be reactive. The future of healthcare must be proactive and continuous. Today a patient presents at an emergency room with a medical condition requiring immediate treatment. However, through the use of smart data gathering technology, the reason for attending the emergency room could have identified well in advance of it becoming urgent. Wearable technology, for instance, similar to a fitbit, could monitor a person's heart-rate, blood pressure or other vital signs and report to a healthcare professional in real time.

Researchers are currently working on using data collected from smartphones or wearable devices that are capable of reporting on speech patterns and motor control. This is aimed at detecting early symptoms of Alzheimer's Disease and Parkinson's. Pill sensors alerting pharmacists as to whether a patient's medications have been taken are also being developed.

These and other advances have enormous benefits for global health. Not only do scientists, researchers and other medical professionals gain important insight into early diagnosis, but also clues into the relationship between varying symptoms. Further development on this front would provide doctors with the ability to identify, treat and potentially cure patients far earlier than would have been the case currently.

These developments will not only save lives, but through early diagnosis and treatment, save an extraordinary amount of money. Take, for instance, what is being referred to as *The Grey Plague* - the increasing cases of dementia and related diseases. Estimates suggest there are currently 50 million people in the world living with dementia. By 2030, the number of cases is expected to increase to 82 million and by 2050, to 131.5 million. In Canada, over 500,000 people are currently living with the disease. By 2038, it is projected to rise to 1.1 million. In addition, for every one person with the disease, one to three others are directly impacted as caregivers. The cost to Canada's economy is currently $15 billion annually and is projected to grow to $153 billion by 2038. The cost to the global economy in 2018, was $1 trillion and will double by 2030.

According to the Alzheimer's Society of Canada, delaying the onset of the disease by 2 years can save the economy $219 billion over three decades. Many people are dismissing the early symptoms of the disease as a function of old age. The implications of this disease will be devastating. If an effective treatment is not found, the cost alone for caring for people with dimentia could potentially bankrupt healthcare systems. Indeed, the amount of capital needed to fund treatment is far beyond the financial capacity of government or the private sector on their own. Either the private market or government is simply not capable of overcoming a challenge of this magnitude. Governments must partner with private industry to continue to press forward toward developing products that will provide preemptive diagnosis.

Any discussion regarding healthcare rarely takes into account the proverbial elephant in the room. The coming crisis in long term care.

There is not a single expenditure in the healthcare portfolio that is increasing faster than long term care. What's more, as the population rapidly ages, these costs are poised to quickly accelerate.

Long term care represents the largest uninsured risk for the aging population. Currently, Japan and Germany are the only countries that have established universal insurance programmes for long term care. Other countries, provide a mix of publicly funded long term care facilities, where waiting lists numbering in the thousands are quite common. In some jurisdictions, there are many who occupy expensive hospital beds because there is no room in any of the publicly funded facilities. This is referred to colloquially as, hallway medicine.

There are also private long term care facilties. The cost of these are anywhere from $5,000 to $7,500 a month depending on location, type of care required or desired amenities. To access these facilities, residents, or their families, are required to cover the costs.

When most people think about their retirement years, they envision playing golf, walking on the beach with their partner, or relaxing at the cottage wallowing away the hours. When their time does come, most assume, it will be quick. Rarely do people consider they may have to live with a chronic illness or disability that would require the assistance of a caregiver let alone be required to live in a long term care facility for years.

Many people are currently struggling just to save enough for retirement. But expected to live longer than any previous generation, the possibility that they will require at least the assistance of a caregiver is fairly high. Of these, some will require care beyond what a caregiver can provide and therefore they will need to be in a institutional style nursing home setting. Saving for a time when care or requiring a nursing home will be necessary, is rarely, if ever taken into consideration when planning post work lives.

It is imperative that governments develop national strategies on how to confront this monumental issue. With 70% of baby boomers expected to require one form of caregiving or another, this issue, if ignored, has the potential to stretch government budgets to the breaking point.

Societies are currently not prepared to cope. The time to act is now. If not, the entire healthcare system will require an urgent trip to the emergency room.

11

Caregiving

With the world's population living longer than ever before, the incidents of dementia and related diseases are expected to dramatically increase in the coming years. So much so, it represents an escalating global health crisis that is on the verge of becoming an epidemic. Estimates suggest there are currently 50 million people living with dementia which constitutes 0.7% of the world's total population. By 2030, cases are expected to increase to 82 million and by 2050 to 131.5 million or 1.4% of the world's population.

Alzheimer's Disease is the most common cause of dementia accounting for approximately 80% of the cases. It is a slow growing neurodegenerative disease for which there is currently no cure. What's more, it is the world's most expensive disease. The UK based organization, Alzheimer's Disease International, has put the global cost of dementia at $818 billion or 1.1% of the world's total GDP. Eighty percent of the total cost associated with treating dementia is the value placed on caring for those afflicted with the disease.

Typically it is family members who find themselves thrust into the position of caring for an aging parent, spouse or partner. Most caregivers never expected they would ever be in such a position. Their lives are suddenly consumed with the responsibility of looking after a parent or partner with what may be the most basic of tasks. They could be responsible for dressing the person they are caring for, preparing and feeding them meals, managing medications and paying bills. In many instances, the caregiver is the only connection the person under care has to the outside world.

Due to the overwhelming physical and emotional demands on the caregiver, the amount, intensity and stress can be overwhelming. On call 24 hours a day, 7 seven days a week, the emotional and physical toll on the caregivers health can be profound. The caregiver's immediate family is placed under increasing stress that could negatively impact relationships with partners and children. Many of these effects are sorely underestimated but nevertheless take a monumental toll on not only the caregiver, the recipient of the care and their family, but also on society and the economy.

According to Statistics Canada, caregivers who provide at least two hours of care per week, reported signs of depression. Sleep disorders, irritability, anger and isolation were also common. As a result, many caregivers experience employment and job related issues. Incidents of physical and emotional abuse by the caregiver are also far too common.

The aging of the population is the most dominant driver leading to increasing need for caregiving. Changing family structures, also a function of an aging population, also have an impact. In recent years, the family structure itself has altered significantly increasing the potential number of people in any one family that may require care. Higher levels of divorce in recent decades have led to multiple step mothers and fathers, grandparents, uncles, aunts and cousins. As the number of family members increase, so to does the potential for caregiving responsibilities increase as well.

The growth of the caregiving economy has far reaching social and cultural implications. Take China, for instance. The consequences of the one child policy and massive urbanization have fundamentally altered China's society. The ancient tradition that the elderly would be taken care of by their children and grandchildren is breaking down. Whereas before the implementation of *The One Child Policy*, couples had numerous children. This meant there were plenty of offspring and grandchildren to look after aging family members. Now, however, that in-house pool of family caregivers is gone. As a result, China has now been forced to adopt a more western style of care model which has given rise to a burgeoning caregiving industry.

Studies have shown that the greatest number of caregivers come from the 45 to 54 year old age segment. These are typically the peak earning years for both men and women. But these same studies also show that the responsibility of caregiving disproportianetly falls on women. So, when it comes to providing care, more women than men are forced to sacrifice their careers.

Women who provide care will typically arrive late for work. They will regularly need to leave early or take time off during the day. Not only do women generally make a lower income than men, once caregiving responsibilities are added on, the deck gets really stacked against them as structural bias kicks in. Fewer hours at work may mean women employees lose health and dental benefits. Employer provided pension, life insurance and prescription drugs may also be lost. A drop in pay will lead to less overall household income which in turn could lead to increasing domestic tensions.

The gender bias worsens. Caregiving responsibilities lead in many instances to sacrificing or getting passed over for career advancement or promotion. This tends to trap women in lower paying jobs. All this results in lower labour market participation by women which in turn reduces the country's overall productivity which impacts the country's overall economic performance.

In a recent CIBC study, they estimate caregivers will have an average amount of $3,300 year in out of pocket expenses. With 2 million Canadians providing care for parents aged 65 and over, this amounts to a cost of over $6 billion to the overall economy. When the study takes into account lost labour and related costs, based on the average wage in Canada, there is a staggering $27 billion in lost income and foregone vacation time.

The impact of caregiving on the caregiver is just one side of the equation. As the size of the workforce diminishes, the available supply of labour becomes more valuable. A simple case of supply and demand. This will lead to a number of challenges ending up on the front door step of employers.

As previously noted, as the population rapidly ages, the incidence of caregiving will also rise. Much of the onus for providing this care will fall on the shoulders of the working age population. With businesses currently sounding the alarm bell because they cannot find enough qualified workers, caregiving will put a further strain on the available pool of labour. For those organizations who have committed to achieving a greater gender balance in their workforce, with fewer women in the available labour pool, this becomes increasingly difficult.

As the need for caregiving increases, the traditional organizational relationship will also change. The post World War II corporate structure which put the needs of the business first, will no longer be viable. As the demographic structure changes, so to does the traditional configuration of business. Historically, organizations invested in constructing ladders for professional growth that reflected the needs of the organization. For these same businesses to attract and retain the workers they will have to design career paths based on the life path of each individual worker. If business does not change to accommodate these life paths, they will jeopardize their very competitiveness by not being able to attract and retain the kinds of skilled workers they so desperately need.

With increasing longevity, there is a need to prepare, educate and train health providers, emergency services, legal and justice system to meet the needs of an older population. Public education is also required so family members will be aware of early signs of dementia and mental illness rather than just chalking it up to unusual behaviour typical of old age. Primary care physicians and other healthcare professionals such as nurses, dentists, pharmacists, dieticians, occupational and physical therapists, religious leaders also require training to spot early signs.

Countries with large multi-ethnic communities, such as Canada, need to have training and public education programmes in a variety of languages. Barriers within ethnic communities that may view mental health issues as something to be kept on the down low, need to know that early detection and treatment is vital for those who may be suffering.

Gender differences must also be acknowledged and respected. Members of the LGBTQ communities should not have to hide who they are when seeking treatment for fear of discrimination. Long term homes need to accommodate people of all genders and not be forced back into the closet.

It was not long ago when one of the dominant social issues was day care for children. It certainly dominated much of the discussion during multiple election campaigns in Canada and other developed countries. The debate over child care is about to be replaced with caring for a parent, family member, friend or neighbour. And if you thought day care for children was a hot political and social potato, compared to caregiving, it will seem like a walk in the park.

12

It's Time To Retire Retirement

During a recent interview with the Globe and Mail newspaper, famed Canadian actor, Christopher Plummer responded to a question as to whether, at the age of 88, he is considering retiring. *Never, never, please!* he said. *I'm terrified to retire. Work just keeps me going.* It sure does. Portraying John Paul Getty in the 2017 movie, *All the Money in the World*, Plummer was nominated for an Oscar. Following that project, he was busy at work portraying Scrooge in *The Man Who Invested Christmas* and also playing Kaiser Wilhelm II in *The Exception*. He certainly gives every indication that he does not have any intention of slowing down anytime soon.

How about Prince Philip, who until recently at age 97, was seen tooling around London in his Land Rover. An accident in early 2019 which resulted in his car flipping on its side has since forced him to put away his driving gloves. Or the late former President of the United States, George H.W. Bush, who celebrated his 90th birthday by skydiving. With a combined age of 294 years, rocker Mick Jagger and his Rolling Stones are still going strong touring throughout the United States and Canada in 2019. Actor Donald Sutherland who is 83, has been hard at work on a new movie coming out in 2019.

For those who prefer to hear about the thrill of athletic competition, there is the Masters Athletics Championships. Many former Olympic athletes take part in this competition to remain active and involved with their sport. One of these Masters' athletes is Singh Sekhon, who is 95 years of age. At the 2018 Canadian Masters Championships, he won 9 gold medals for placing first in the pentathlon for men 90 to 99 years, the shot put, javelin throw, hammer throw, discus and weight throw events. He also won gold in the 100, 200 and 400 metre dashes for men 95 years and over. In the process, he set three Canadian outdoor championship records. He is now in training for the next set of championships set to take place in 2020.

The concept of retirement is a fairly modern development. Throughout most of human history, people would work until either they just couldn't physically do so any longer, or they died. Over the last sixty years, it was commonplace for most upon graduation from either high school or a post secondary institution, to work for a single company for their entire career. Job security meant a decent wage, providing enough to purchase a three bedroom bungalow in the suburbs, a car and to enjoy a two or three week family vacation each summer. Most importantly, it meant good pay and a secure retirement income through a defined benefit pension plan where the employer assumed all the risk.

Imagine in your mind's eye the following which was very common in offices across the developed world throughout the 1950s and 1960s. All the employees, whether in an office or on the shop floor, are gathered around chanting *for he's a jolly good fellow, for he's a jolly good fellow, that nobody can deny.* There's a retirement cake that gets clumsily cut up by your assistant, Marg, who after placing each piece on a paper plate licks the excess icing off her fingers. A white plastic fork is added and passed around until everyone has a slice. The head of the company would come down to deliver brief, yet sentimental remarks about your loyalty and dedication to the company over the last forty years and how much you will be missed. You receive a plaque with the company logo emblazoned across the top and your name indicating all your years of loyal service. At this point, Marg gets all choked up and others begin to shed a tear or two. Then comes the *piece de resistance*. To celebrate the next phase of your life, *the golden years*, you are presented with a gold watch. The accompanying card, signed by everyone, reads: *You gave us your time. Now, we are giving you ours.*

Then the long walk to the exit for the last time. Along the way, you would be embraced by colleagues for the proverbial goodbye hug accompanied by a slap on the back. They all wish you good luck and to enjoy your retirement *you lucky s.o.b.* With your bankers box in toe containing your four decades of memories, family pictures and nic naks picked up on business trips over the years, you wave goodbye to Frank, the security guard. You hand in your company identification card and then head out to the parking lot. Open your trunk, place the bankers box in, take one last look at the building where you spent the better part of your life. Give a little snicker and off you go into the sunset of retirement. Secure in the knowledge that you would be receiving your monthly lifetime defined benefit pension plan payment and state pension. Both of these would provide enough retirement income for you and your wife to live out your remaining years in comfort and financial security.

Today's retirement reality is far from this idyllic picture. Yet, it seems so ingrained in our minds. Like it's always been that way. Where did it come from?

The concept of retirement itself can be traced as far back as the first century B.C. Roman emperor, Augustus, permitted veterans of the Imperial Roman army the opportunity to retire from active service and hang up their armour. Included was the payment of a one time stipend, or pension, for those who had served a minimum number of years.

After the fall of the Roman empire, retirement disappeared with it. It was not until the later half of the 19th century, that retirement would re-appear. As Marxism began to spread through the Germanic states, Prussian Chancellor, Otto von Bismarck, who is credited with unifying the states into a single country, in order to curry favour with the working class, proposed that once a worker reached the age of 70, they could retire from their job and receive a state pension. The proposal was successful in winning the favour of workers even though few people lived to 70 years at that time.

In 1916, the German Reichstag lowered the age to qualify for the state pension to 65. Countries that subsequently followed Germany's lead, would also adopt 65 years as the threshold. Even to this very day, the age of 65, give or take a year or two, it is still in use even though average life expectancy globally has increased by approximately three decades since Bismarck's day.

Workers throughout the developed world always believed that if they work hard they would be able to enjoy the final stage of their life relaxing, travelling and spending time with family and friends. Financial support would come from personal savings, pension from employment and old age security benefits provided by government.

However, current studies show that as more people reach retirement age they do not have enough money saved nor do they have a pension from their employer. This leaves the state provided pension, which was never meant to be an income replacement for people in old age. It is a social programme, designed to supplement savings and other income streams. The great fear is that millions of middle class people will end up retiring into poverty having to rely solely on their monthly social security payment to survive.

In the early 1990s, with inflation low and the expectation it would stay there, central banks followed a low interest rate policy to encourage demand for housing. It worked. Demand for homes increased. But this also drove demand in other areas as well which in turn led to increasing personal indebtedness. Canadians, who traditionally had a reputation as a nation of savers, purchased larger and larger homes. First time buyers came into the market. As well, speculation ran wild. All these occurrences increased personal debt levels to record high levels.

In 2008, in the wake of the global financial crisis, to stimulate growth, central banks cut rates further. Zero and negative rate values were not uncommon. Debt levels increased even more. On the rise for the past three decades, household debt in Canada is currently over $2 trillion. Put another way, each Canadian owes $1.70 for every dollar of net disposable income. The one time nation of savers, has now become a nation of debtors.

What's more disturbing, according to Statistics Canada, Canadians in the age group 55 to 64, some 74% are carrying debt which represents a 60% increase from 1999. For those 65 years and over, only 27% had debt in 1999. By 2016, it had increased to 42%. This means that at least half of the Canadians who are retiring are doing so carrying some amount of debt. Surely these people are concerned more about paying off outstanding debt than saving for retirement.

A 2018 CIBC study reported that Canadians believed they will need $756,000 for retirement. However, the average amount currently saved by Canadians is $184,000, a far cry from what they believe they will need. Some 90% of Canadians had no formal plan on how to reach the amount they will need for retirement. Among this group, those 55 years of age and over, 43% of men and 27% of women, did not have a plan at all. Most believe they will live on their Old Age Security benefits and Canada Pension Plan.

More staggering, was that almost 40% indicated they haven't even thought about retirement and even if they have, they are just unable to save anything at all. One third of baby boomers up to the age of 64, have not saved anything. Other studies have revealed similar findings.

According to a 2016 global survey conducted by HSBC regarding people's attitudes about retirement, 80% of respondents were in favour of eliminating the whole concept of retirement altogether. In fact, 75% wanted to keep working well past their country's retirement age.

As people live longer, retirement has come to be seen as just another stage in the life cycle. An opportunity to re-invent themselves. Go back to school, travel or change careers. After all, people are living longer, healthier lives than ever before in human history. Living another twenty or thirty years past the age of 65 is no longer a rarity. For the tens of thousands of baby boomers who are turning 65 every day around the world, they are not ready to call it a day. This is the generation, after all, that has spearheaded change from the time they first appeared on the scene following the end of the Second World War.

Although for some who plan on working past 65, they will be doing so because they need to. For a lot of people, through no fault of their own, they were just unable to save enough. They need to continue working because they have to pay for housing, food and basic neccessities. The idea of not working is just not an option.

In a world where change is constant. Where technology is advancing by leaps and bounds. Where everyone wants the latest gadget or tech toy, it seems odd that anyone would want to hold on to a relic from over a century ago. Holding on to a retirement age that is rooted in a by-gone era where sweat shops, back breaking work and life threatening conditions were the norm, retirement made a lot of sense. But contemporary working conditions no longer resemble the shop floors of the early decades of the industrial revolution.

Age, like the value of money, should be adjusted over time. When Germany's government decided in 1916 to make 65 the age to qualify for their state retirement pension, average life expectancy was 47. Using the same age of 65 today when average life expectancy is 83, does not make any sense. The price of a gallon of gas in Toronto in 1916, was approximately 15 cents. In 2019, that same 15 cents has a value of $3.46. With an increase in life expectancy, the same principle should be applied to age as with money.

Ever hear someone say, 65 is the new 55 or 55 is the new 45? Well, that what it means. Age should be adjusted for the increase in life spans to take into account today's longer life expectancies. In fact, if the *retirement age* matched the increases in life expectancy, the current challenge would be ameliorated to some extent.

Keep in mind that more than a century has passed since 65 years was arbitrarily chosen as the retirement age. The whole concept behind selecting 65 was to make sure that more money would be collected in taxes from the working age population than would be paid out. Not very sophisticated, yet effective acturarial rationale.

However, although life expectancy has increased by three decades since 1916, the retirement age of 65 has, at most, increased by a year or two. But herein lies the challenge. Population pyramids are inverting. When 65 was selected, it's doubtful any consideration was given to some point in the future when average life expectancy would exceed the state's retirement age. They did not have any reason to believe that there would be a new age distribution and that new capacity would be necessary. But, surprise! That day has arrived.

Working age populations are diminishing in all industrialized countries. The size of the workforce needs to be expanded, not contracted. Incentivizing people who are capable of and want to continue working past 65 years, should be encouraged. As people live longer, healthier lives, they should be emboldened to stay in the workforce for as long as they wish. It is only by expanding the size of the workforce will capacity increase thereby increasing productivity. This will keep the economy competitive giving it the strength to withstand future shocks.

In today's fiercely competitive global market, business cannot risk being short sighted. Immediate savings on salaries and wages should not come at the expense of creating a brain drain of experienced workers. It is a time to retain the best and the brightest. Employers need to prioritize succession, training and mentoring programmes rather than merely replace older employees with younger, less expensive and inexperienced versions.

The empirical evidence is clear. Studies have shown time and time again, that an age diverse workforce is far more productive than one consisting of single generation or two. Not only will an age diverse workforce be more productive, but it is the quickest fix to building new capacity to ensure the sustainability of healthcare and social safety infrastructures.

The time has come to retire retirement.

13

Ah Look At All The Lonely People

With the growing interconnectedness of technology via social media, face time, text messaging, and talking on smart phones, it would defy logic at some level to think that anyone can ever feel alone. For those who live in big cities it means potentially seeing thousands of people a day on public transit, walking on the street or going to a shopping mall. Even for those who live in small rural areas a walk along the town's main street would mean running into neighbours and friends. Yet, many people live isolated and solitary existences.

Isolation and loneliness is a very serious problem facing people of all ages. No age group is immune. Feelings of loneliness and isolation among younger adults tends to be more episodic in nature and a feeling of *not fitting in* with contemporaries. This may be a result of being placed in a new environment, such as a school, being a victim of bullying, or perhaps possessing language or a cultural barrier. Usually, once the external variable causing the feeling of loneliness or isolation is removed, so to do the negative feelings.

Much of the empirical evidence to date demonstrates that loneliness and isolation are conditions that tend to present most in the population at two stages in the average life span. It peaks in mid-teens, tails off and then consistently tracks a linear path until older age when it increases once again. However, the increase in incidents reported later in life are caused by a very different set of circumstances with a far different effect.

The data reveals that large numbers of older Canadians feel they are socially isolated. For those 65 years of age and over, some 20% fall in this category. By the time they reach 80 years of age, feelings of loneliness and isolation increase to 80%. Similar figures are recorded in most other developed countries as well.

These numbers are expected to rapidly increase in the coming years. With increasing life expectancy, older Canadians, particularly those in the baby boom generation, place a high premium on being socially connected and physically active. However, as people grow older, their life undergoes serious change. For each person, these changes occur at different ages. But as the evidence demonstrates, some four-out-of-five older adults will experience feelings of loneliness and isolation by the time they reach 80 years.

Workplace retirement, the death of a spouse, family member or friends, the development of an illnesses or disability, or loss of a driver's license, are just some of the triggers that result in older adults developing feelings of loneliness and isolation. Fewer family and friends means less social interaction and the loss of a once relied upon support system. Studies show that the lack of a social network is linked to a 60% increase in the risk of cognitive decline.

An increase in the number of Canadians forced to cope with a chronic illness also increases with age. According to Statistics Canada's 2014 Community Health Survey, 30% of Canadians 65 to 79 years of age and 38% of those 80 years and over, reported having two or more chronic conditions. The most common are hypertension, arthritis and diabetes.

In addition, according to the 2013 Canadian Survey on Disability, over one-third of Canadians aged 65 and over live with a disability. For those over 75 years, those with a disability increases to 42.5%. These and other ailments make it difficult to perform tasks which at one time they could do with ease, such as walking up steps, bathing or shopping. These illnesses can take a huge toll on a persons quality of life, independence and pride.

In addition to the pain and discomfort associated with these diseases, is the stigma associated with having one or more of these illnesses. Notwithstanding the effect it has on their own level of self-confidence, it is becoming all too common for those suffering from an illness to be marginalized, ignored and even abandoned by family and friends. There are also what is referred to as, elder orphans. These are elderly people who do not have any family or friends or support network whatsoever.

There are also additional groups of older adults who are identified as having increased risk of social isolation. These include the following: Older Canadians with a physical or mental disability, low income older adults, older aged caregivers, Aboriginal peoples, residents of rural communities, new Canadians and those who identify as LGBTQ.

As the average life expectancy of Canadians continues to increase, so to will the number of those who suffer in silence from loneliness and isolation. Regardless, no matter the reason, these triggers will leave a person feeling vulnerable and emotionally exposed. Studies show that this in turn leads to depression and melancholy which in turn leads to diminishing physical health and well being. This in turn leads many to neglect their health by starting to smoke, drink or not take prescribed medication.

The Canadian Institute for Health Information report that 44% of seniors living in residential care have been diagnosed with depression. What's more, men over the age of 80 years have among the highest suicide rates of all age groups. It's a vicious circle because poor health leads to further loss of self esteem and poorer emotional health which in turn leads to worse physical health.

Brigham Young University psychologist, Julianne Holt-Lunstad, who has conducted the largest ever review into loneliness, says: *It's comparable to smoking up to 15 cigarettes a day. It exceeds the risk of alcohol consumption, it exceeds the risk of physical inactivity, obesity and it exceeds the risk of air pollution.* This has led many in the global health community to declare that loneliness and isolation have moved well beyond being a public health crisis to the point where it is now, an epidemic.

The irony of this crisis is found in the movement in recent decades for older persons to *ageing in place*. Based on a theory developed by environmental gerontologists, it maintains that as people age, they are increasingly attached to the place where they live. The concept of *aging in place* has become popular for two reasons. First, it allows the older person to remain in their home for as long as they are able. This provides a feeling of security, independence and control feared lost if they were to move into an institutional setting. Second, government prefers the aging in place alternative to public institutional care because it is far less costly.

Ideally, for an older person to age in place, their home environment needs to be made more functional. Typically, this would mean installation of hand grips, replacement of round door knobs with levers and other retrofits. When a caregiver is needed, structural modifications to create separate sleeping and living quarters may be required. For many, this may cause financial hardship. For others who live in rental accommodation, any changes to the apartment unit may pose emotional distress if there is an uncooperative landlord.

Notwithstanding the many advantages attributed to aging in place are for those who live alone. Those who do, as is the case with 25% of Canadians 65 years and over, they are far more likely to endure loneliness and isolation. This is much more of an issue for women than for men. One-third of women in Canada 65 years and over live alone compared to 16% of men. Although incidences of loneliness do present in shared facilities, such as nursing homes, chronic care and long term care hospitals and seniors' residences, for those who age in place, the incidence are far greater.

Isolation and loneliness among the elderly is a growing problem that is in desparate need of a solution. A number of different approaches have been taken by governments and non-governmental organizations in an attempt to solve this crisis. In the United States, Lance Robertson, Assistant Secretary for Aging, has a long history of working on behalf of older persons and the disabled in Oklahoma. His plan is to expand faith-based partnerships as a way of combating isolation among older Americans. In Japan, which has the world's oldest population, loneliness is a big problem. To service many of those who feel lonely, there are now organizations where one can *rent a friend* for a day, week or even longer.

The most ambitious and boldest effort to date, can be found in the UK. In response to the 2017 Cox Report on Loneliness, the following year, the government established a Minister for Loneliness. In establishing the position, Prime Minister Theresa May said: *I want to confront this challenge for our society and for all of us to take action to address the loneliness endured by the elderly, by carers, by those who have lost loved ones - people who have no one to talk to or share their thoughts and experiences with.*

The creation of a Minister who's sole responsibility it is to make sure the voice of the lonely and isolated are heard at the cabinet table is certainly a laudable initiative. The UK government should be applauded for doing so. Naturally, it is far too early to gauge the effectiveness of this initiative and whether it should be considered by other governments. Nevertheless, it demonstrates the seriousness with which it takes this issue is taken in the UK and for that reason alone should be closely monitored by policy makers in other jurisdictions.

Other initiatives are currently underway in different countries. No matter how aggressive and well intentioned any programme may be to reduce loneliness and isolation, what is clear is that it will not be solved quickly. It is a process that will take time. To find this solution is not the sole responsibility of government, business or civil society. Rather, it will require a partnership between all facets of society working hand in hand towards a goal of eradicating what is rapidly becoming a global crisis.

One thing for sure, the economic costs of loneliness and isolation are deep.

Older Canadians who are isolated experience a four to five times greater risk of hospitalization. Those who live alone are also at greater risk of elder abuse, fraud and scams.

Psychologists say that loneliness can be more dangerous to one's physical health than diabetes and obesity. It is linked to high blood pressure, dementia and increased morbidity. For those who live alone, they have increased risks of developing illnesses related to even mundane and everyday activities such as sleeping. Obstructive sleep apnea, an uncontrollable blockage in the asophygas when the soft tissues in the throat collapse during sleep, is difficult to detect when one sleeps on their own. Sleep apnea can lead to coronary issues and a host of other serious ailments if it goes undiagnosed.

Studies have shown how loneliness and isolation lead to altered immune systems, increased levels of stress, high blood pressure, heart disease, increased levels of cognitive decline and stroke. It has also been found that isolated persons are twice as likely to die prematurely than those who are not.

In addition to emotional and physical illnesses, an older person who lives alone and without much social interaction, something as eminently treatable as a fractured bone can become a life threatening occurrence. In fact, in Canada, the United States and Great Britan some 25% older people die as a result of falling and fracturing their leg. Without a family member, friend, room mate or visitor around to help, the injured person is left waiting while writhing in pain for either someone to show up or attempt to contact emergency services themselves.

The Silver Line, is a 24 hour a day help line in the UK that is a service that provides older people with someone to speak to if they are feeling lonely. The service accepts some 1,600 calls each day. They also have a team of volunteers who correspond via letter with elders all around the UK. Silver Circles is another service that conducts group calls on the telephone each week.

Isolation and loneliness are very serious problems for older adults. Partners and friends become ill or even die. As people age, they become less mobile, lose their hearing and their vision could become impaired. Plus a host of other physical and emotional issues arise. Studies show that people who are isolated tend to suffer more from illness, depression and even die earlier than those who have social interaction. Loneliness and isolation is a growing problem. Any solution will require cooperation between all levels of government, business and civil society.

14

Aged Population Canadian Style

January 1, 1946, the first new year's day since 1940, that the world was not embroiled in war. It also marked the beginning of a new era. For the next eighteen years, in Canada and most other countries, was the start of the largest baby boom in global history. After living through the Great Depression, fighting a world war to make the world safe for democracy, giving birth to a new generation was the ultimate expression of optimism for mankind's collective future. For their bravery, courage and hope, they are known as the greatest generation.

When speaking of the baby boom generation, most are refering to the 76 million Americans and 9 million Canadians born between the years 1946 and 1965. However, the actual post war baby boom generation was far more widespread. The UK, France and Austria had the biggest baby boom in Europe. The Nordic countries similarly had a large number of births as did Asia and most of Latin America. However, most of the attention in the literature focuses on the baby boom generation in North America.

In both the United States and Canada, the parents of baby boomers were the epitome of the traditional family structure. The average age men married at was 21. For women, it was 20. The majority of these couples had their first child by nine months. When the baby boom generation ended in 1965, the average number of births per family was 3.2.

From the first days they appeared on the scene it became evident that the baby boomers were not going to be like any other generation that came before them. The baby boomers would come to lead the greatest change in consumer, social, economic and political trends, attitudes and culture than any generation before them or any generation since. They became a core marketing demographic for just about every product. Even today, the baby boom generation continues to blaze new trails, change old practices and viewpoints, and lead societal change.

Even as infants, their influence was unprecedented. Initially, they were responsible for the unprecedented growth of baby products such as diapers, ointments and creams. Those in the medical profession and trained in pediatrics had more patients than they had time. Toys of every shape, size and model could not get on to store shelves fast enough. This rapidly growing generation of infants needed to be fed, clothed and entertained.

As they aged into their teens, boomers were the first generation to possess significant spending power. Products were developed that appealed to the baby boomers as they became teenagers and had money to spend. It was not long into the 1950s, that the baby boom generation had become the dominant demographic force in history. To the delight of those with something to sell to this generation, it was just the beginning.

On every sandlot in the United States at this time, young boys imagined they were Mickey Mantle or Jackie Robinson when they got up to home plate in little league. Young girls in both Canada and the United States were hooked on a new doll just released by

Mattel Corporation called, Barbie. It came with all different sorts of outfits. She was always ready for any occassion.

In Canada, cold winters gave rise to what would become a right of passage for every young boy. Road hockey.

It was never too cold to rally the kids in the neighbourhood for a game. For those too young to play, they would provide their commentary in their best Danny Gallivan or Bill Hewitt voice. *A cannonading drive, making their way gingerly over the centre red line* or *the puck is lassoed into the other team's end*, were repeated time and time again. When a car would was seen making its way in the direction of the game, someone would scream CAR!. The nets were moved off to the side until it passed. Then the game resumed. Most Canadian men in their fifties to mid seventies recall these moments vividly in their mind's eye.

A generation of boys that seemed like they were making endless trips by bicycle to the neighbourhood variety store to pick up a jug of milk for mom. Many times it would require a second trip because on your way home the jug would somehow break off the handle bars and splatter all over the ground. If you had not used the extra 10 cents you were given to buy candy, gum or a lola, you could just ride back to the store and buy another jug. But, what self respecting kid didn't use that extra ten cents to load up on at least a pack of hockey or baseball cards. That meant coming clean when you got home and having to fess up and explain how the candy or gum all seemed to make it back in one piece, but not the milk. No matter, reluctantly, another trip would just have to be made. However, this time, mom wanted all the change.

For the leading edge of this generation, January 1, 2011, marked the first day a baby boomer turned 65 years of age and became eligible to receive their monthly Old Age Security payment. From that point on, beginning 1/1/11 and every day until

December 31, 2030, an average of 1,000 baby boomers will turn 65 years of age in Canada. As a point of comparison, in the United States, 10,000 baby boomers are turning 65 every day.

Another date of note, May 2, 2017, when Statistics Canada announced, based on the results of the previous year's census, for the first time in the country's history, the number of Canadians 65 years of age and over, were greater in number than those aged fifteen years and under. The data revealed there were 5.9 million Canadians 65 years and over and 5.8 million under fifteen years. Although the overall population increased by some 5%, there was a 20% jump in the share of the population that was 65 years of age and over. What's more, the data also showed there was an increase of 19% in the number of Canadians 85 years and over and a 41% increase among those over 100 years of age. The median age, the age at which exactly half the total population is above and half below, had increased by six months to 41.2 years from the 2011 census.

MORE SENIORS THAN CHILDREN

In 2016, for the first time, the share of seniors (16.9%) exceeded the share of children (16.6%).

PERCENTAGE OF THE TOTAL POPULATION

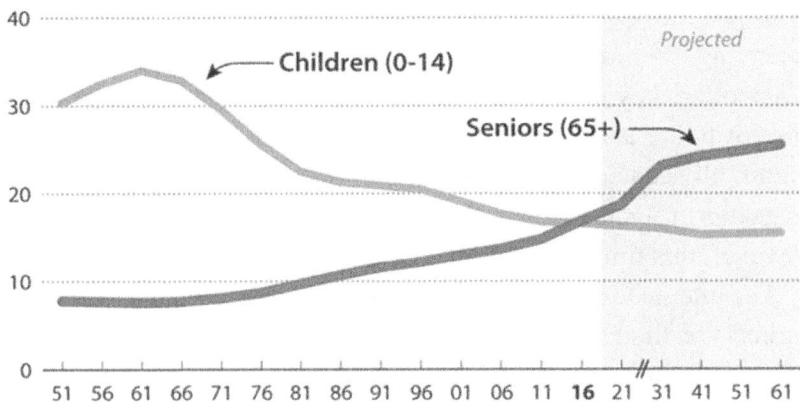

SOURCE: STATISTICS CANADA THE CANADIAN PRESS

What is more striking about this data, are the trend lines. Current projections indicate that by 2031, the proportion of Canadians 65 years of age and over will increase to slightly under 30% of the country's population. This will place Canada in the dubious company of those countries with some of the oldest populations in the world.

There are a number of factors that are accelerating the rapid pace at which Canada's population is aging. Most significantly, thanks to advances in medicine, healthcare and lifestyle, Canadians are living longer than ever before. Average life expectancy has been increasing in Canada at a fairly rapid clip over the last one hundred years. In 1921, the average life expectancy for a Canadian was slightly over fifty seven years. A half century later, in 1971, the average life expectancy had increased to 71 years. By 2018, another twelve years was added taking it to 83 years. Canada enjoys one of the longest life expectancies in the world.

Canada had a particularly large baby boom after the end of the Second World War. Between the years 1946 and 1965, there were 8.2 million, or 412,000 per month, babies born in Canada. The fertility rate was 3.7 per woman. These numbers have been buffetted by robust levels of immigration since the 1980s. As of today, there are 9.6 million baby boomers in Canada representing 29% of the country's total population.

Due to the social and cultural changes beginning in the 1960s, the age at which women started to give birth was on the rise. The average age for women who gave birth during the years 1946 to 1965, was 24. By the mid 1970s, however, this age was on the rise. In fact, at an average of 30 years, it was returning to levels which were prevalent before the baby boom began. In addition to giving birth later than their parents, the baby boomers were also having far fewer children.

From it's peak fertility rate of 3.94 children per woman in 1959, by 1965, it had dropped to 3.16. This marked the end of the baby boom. By the latter half of the 1960s, with the influence of religion waning, easier access to divorce and the increased availability of effective forms of contraception, the fertility rate fell well below the replacement value of 2.1. It has never fully recovered to anywhere near its peak. The rate currently stands at 1.67.

There are certainly a host of different responsibilities and expectations on a government when the average life expectancy of its population is 60 as opposed to when it is 80. Extended life spans will produce significant economic changes, increasing health and social programme expenditures and certainly profound changes to every other aspect of society. As recently as 2016, the Chair of Canada's Advisory Council on Economic Growth, Dominic Barton, stated:

One of the biggest worries we have is we are a very aging population in Canada. If we don't get on it, we are going to have some big difficulty.

The media also made their opinion's known. Here are some of the stories that ran in a some of Canada's news outlets:

Canada woefully unprepared to deal with senior population surge, Global News, May 30, 2017
Canada is not ready for the needs of its aging population, Hamilton Spectator, April 17, 2018
Canada's aging population is going to put a serious strain on government coffers, Maclean's, October 31, 2017

People are not only living longer but they are looking, acting and feeling better than ever before in human history. However, increasing life spans are posing some challenges. Current welfare state programmes, such as, Old Age Security, universal healthcare and other age related social expenditures, are quickly growing out of sync with a life course that does not match up with current demographic realities.

Even within Canada, there are regions that are aging much faster than others. Founded as a federation, Canada's vast land mass and unequal development created areas of the country that required support from more prosperous regions. To address these concerns, the government of Canada established a Royal Commission on Dominion (Federal) - Provincial Relations. Reporting to Parliament in 1940, the Rowell-Sirois Commission, as it is more commonly known, recommended addressing the country's vertical fiscal imbalance. A system of equalization payments were established in 1957, designed to compensate those provinces that were experiencing fiscal deficiencies. Based on the principle of a national standard, defined as the fiscal capacity of all ten provinces, it was established that each province would have equal revenue raising capacity.

Since its introduction, the programme has seen its share of criticism. Premiers have referred to it as unfair, inequitable and flawed and have called for fundamental changes. Some have levelled criticism against the programme for penalizing those provinces that grow their economy and are forced to pay for another province's underperformance. A common criticism is the whole process has become far too political and has strayed from its original intent.

Determining uniform national standards have consistently been a bone of contention. At times leading to some very strained relations between the federal, provincial and territorial governments. The aging of Canada's population is exacerbating these tensions.

In a country with a land mass as large as Canada's, there have been times in the country's history when the economy of one region outperforms others. This tends to result in a migration of young working age people to those provinces or regions where the economy is prospering. A diminishing workforce in the originating region will lead to the narrowing of dependency ratios resulting in mounting fiscal stress. Additionally, Canada's equalization formula will call on the prospering province to contribute to making up for lost fiscal capacity of the provinces whose economies are not performing as well. Disparate economic performance leads to making an uneven population distribution all that much worse. For instance, over the last four decades, the Atlantic provinces have gone from having Canada's lowest median age to it's highest. In addition, three out of the four provinces, with the exception of Prince Edward Island, have declining populations. As the working age population leaves for greener pastures, left behind is an older age segment. With a diminishing workforce, the challenges posed by population aging are made much more acute and the fiscal challenges far more urgent.

Many see the current equalization formula as far too unequal. They may have a point. Particularly when the formula is being fuelled by a population that is rapidly aging unevenly across the country. There are some who advocate for changing the formula to include a needs assessment. In other words, determining payment based more on the salient demographic requirements of a province.

The debate over equalization is as old as the programme itself which began in 1957. Implemented to provide a fiscal mechanism to strengthen national unity, it has, at times, served to increase tensions between regions. One thing is certain, as long as Canada has unequal distribution of resources, the country will have an economy that is uneven across regions. As always, this has resulted in population retention issues. But in the past when this occured, the shifting fortunes of the regional economies could be relied upon to iron out these differences over time. However, with Canada's population rapidly aging, some regions may just run out of an adequate amount of runway space this time around.

At the national level, Canada's rapidly aging population is a cause for great concern. As a result of a comparatively large baby boom population followed by a fertility rate well below replacement, Canada's old age dependency ratio has been rapidly tightening. In fact, it is falling faster than most other OECD member countries.

As recently as 1970, the country's dependency ratio was a robust 9 to 1. Nine Canadians employed for every one 65 years of age and over. However, over the course of the five decades, Canada's working age population has been rapidly falling. Currently, the old age dependency ratio is at 4.7 to 1. By 2030, it is projected to drop to an alarming 2.5 to 1.

In order to increase the numbers in the working age population, some have suggested that Canada should increase its level of immigration. Although this should surely be done in any event, it will not, however, do much to slow the overall aging of the population. Remember, immigrants age too. Unless millions of young teens are admitted without their parents, which is certainly unconscionable, it will do little by way of leading to a comprehensive solution.

The default position of most governments has been to increase taxes, run budgetary deficits and/or cut benefits. Although as distasteful as each of these options are to governments, it is what they have resorted to rather than undertake fundamental policy change. But there comes a point where increasing levels of taxation could reach a tipping point. Too much taxation could cause a brain drain of young talent to flee jurisdictions where taxation levels are lower. This in turn would lead to a diminishing workforce which leads to decreasing levels of productivity and growth, economic opportunity and career advancement.

Keep in mind that the implications of population aging are transformative. Likewise, so too must the policy response. Buying time by increasing taxes, running up deficit spending or reducing benefits, is pushing off these decisions to some future government. However, in the meantime, as the population continues to rapidly age, governments run the risk of getting caught up in negative economic headwinds which have their origin elsewhere. Deep debt and big deficits will limit a government's ability to effectively respond to an urgent threat. Therefore, it is imperative that governments make these important policy changes now. Not doing so serves to increase the country's fiscal risk level by limiting it's policy options in the future.

As Canada's population continues to rapidly age and the dependency ratio drops to levels that will jeopardize the sustainability of current public expenditure models, there is an urgent need to begin to re-think the basic assumptions that form the foundation of the country's transfer models. The sustainability of Canada's health-care and social systems will depend on the building of new capacity. This will require re-configuring current dependency based transfer models with an eye to expanding the pool of available workers. It would also serve to recognize certain prevailing facts.

According to a TD Bank Group survey from January 2019, a staggering 64% of Canadians have very little saved for retirement. The respondents also indicated that they will need to work past turning 65 because they will not have enough savings. Most find their current day to day financial demands simply too onerous and are finding it next to impossible to save for retirement.

For many more of today's seniors, for those capable of doing so, are working. According to Statistics Canada, 20% of Canadians 65 years and over are working. This is a 100% increase from just 1995. What's more, the trend lines are also showing that these numbers will continue to go up. Also rapidly increasing, is the number of Canadian men 70 years and over who are working. It is currently at 33%. With Canada's 65 years and over population poised to double by 2036, there is growing concern that after decades of reducing rates of poverty among the elderly, the trend may be reversing.

In 2018, according to a study conducted by TransUnion, mortgages issued to those aged 73 to 93 increased by 63% from the previous year. The report also showed an increase of 18% for those aged 54 to 72. These increases could be to assist children or grandchildren with the purchase of their own homes. That is possible. But it is more likely that many of them simply need the money to live on because their own savings have been exhausted.

So, what are some solutions?

Well, for starters, instead of incentivizing Canadians to retire at 65, they should be encouraged to keep working. That is for those who are able to do so. After all, most are remaining in the workforce anyways. Some are choosing to transition into a easier lifestyle.

This does not mean eliminating retirement altogether. The option of leaving the workforce at 65, 67 or 70, should be a personal choice. For those who have been in physically or emotionally demanding work, they should certainly have that option. But with an average life expectancy currently at 83 years, Canadians should be permitted to postpone receiving their Old Age Security and Canada Pension Plan benefits for as long as they wish.

Another compelling reason for encouraging Canadians to remain in the workforce past 65 years, is the flip side of the reason that brought them into it in the first place. Canada boasted fairly good growth rates going back to the 1970s due to an increase in the size of the workforce. A big part of this increase was a result of women entering the labour market. Well, as this generation hits 65 years of age at the rate of 1,000 a day in Canada, the shock to the economy if they leave the workforce as quickly as they arrived, could seriously impact already challenged productivity levels.

To reduce the shock of a large exodus of well educated, experienced and skilled workers from the labour market, some countries have decided to increase their so-called retirement age. The age in the United Kingdom, for instance, currently at 65 for men and 60 for women, will be increasing to 66 for both sexes in 2020. Australia is going from 65.5 years to 67 by 2023. Russia will be increasing from its current qualifying age of 60 for men and 55 for women to 65 and 60 respectively.

Increasing the age to qualify for a public old aged pension is effective in immediately expanding the supply of labour. It would also slow down the pace at which a country's dependency ratio is falling.

With one of the highest standards of living of any country, Canada is the envy of the world. That must never change. But as the population ages at an accelerating pace, Canada must take substantive policy action preferably much sooner rather than later. Policy makers currently have an opportunity to explore new and innovative solutions to meet the challenges an aging population poses. Canada could stand as a model to the world.

One thing is certain. Undertaking bold action now will serve to sustain both the quantity and quality of Canada's healthcare, social programmes and other age related expenditures every Canadian is so proud of. However, relying on a population structure built on an assumption where there are far greater numbers of young people of working age to support growing numbers of an older dependent population, is just not sustainable. Policy makers and all Canadians have a vested interested in ensuring that the Canada left to future generations, is at least as economically prosperous and socially just as the current generation inherited itself. Anything less, would be a betrayal of Canada's fundamental values of social justice and common destiny.

15

The Changing Political
And Social Landscape

According to conventional wisdom, the older an individual gets, the more conservative they become. If this is in fact the case, with an overwhelming number of the population 65 years and over, conservatism has a bright political future.

However, the baby boomers, born following World War Two, best remembered for their mistrust of the establishment, may be an exception to the rule. Don't trust anyone over thirty! was their battle cry. Coming of age in the 1960s, this was the generation of sex, drugs and rock 'n roll. They were the generation that fought for civil rights, women's rights, gay rights, and to end the war in Vietnam. Today's environmental movement can trace its roots to this era when the baby boomers spoke about ecology and taking better care of the world's land and water. They were, as the Buffalo Springfield song goes, *Young people speaking their minds*.

A generation that celebrated alternative lifestyles. This included the use of marijuana and other halucenegetic drugs such as heroin and LSD. Turn on, tune in, drop out, was more than just a slogan but a way of life. The phrase first coined in 1967 by Timothy Leary, a counter culture guru, along with others such as Abbie Hoffman, Jerry Rubin, and Eldrige Cleaver, were the pied pipers of a generation coming of age in the turbulent 1960s. They advocated flower power and to make love, not war.

No generation in history rocked society to its very core and is responsible for such profound change as the baby boomers. If there is a possibility of a generation breaking from convention and not end up adopting conservative values as others did before them, it is certainly the baby boomers.

However, within a decade this same generation that were protesting in the streets, had appeared to grow remarkably conservative. The hippie generation had become the Yuppie generation. This same generation of young people that castigated Ronald Reagan, referring to him Ray-Gun, for his support of the Vietnam War, when he was the Republican governor of California from 1967 to 1975, overwhelmingly supported his candidacy for President of the United States in 1980 and for re-election in 1984.

Polling in 1980 and 1984, consistently showed that a majority of those 27 to 38 years of age, supported Ronald Reagan, who at the time was considered by many as too conservative even for mainstream Republicans. One is reminded of the old addage: If you're not a socialist when you are twenty, you have no heart and if you are not a capitalist by the time you are thirty, you have no head. With aging comes responsibility such as a mortgage payments, earning a living and even raising a family. Youthful optimism and idealism is suddenly challenged and in it's place responsibility, productivity and careful planning rule the day.

The turn to conservatism among the baby boom generation was not only in the United States. The U.K. elected conservative Margaret Thatcher as Prime Minister in 1979. Canada had a short flirtation with a minority Conservative government in 1979. It was not until 1984, that Canada would elect a Conservative majority government that would govern for the next nine years.

So what does this mean for the political landscape? Will the aging baby boomers also be as conservative as their predecessors? These are all good questions. Unfortunately, so far, they remained unanswered. Remember, there is no precedent for a society where the majority of voters are 65 years of age and over. This is unchartered territory. Perhaps older voters will organize and advocate for issues of common interest. Or, maybe they will find more common ground on issues that have nothing to do with their age. This is a very individualistic oriented generation, after all.

Politics could very well be on the cusp of profound strategic realignment. As the distribution of the population changes so to will interests. The left will need to re-evaluate their defense of dependency based health and social care models. The future sustainability of these programmes are in increasing jeopardy due to declining working age populations which serve as their backbone. Similarly, those on the right will have to offer more than mere fiscal restraint and balanced budgets. They will need to offer a vision of how to care for the aging members of society.

New voting blocs could very well be created that could lead to monumental political change. As voters, the baby boom generation are wild cards as they age. No one can predict where it will all lead but one thing is for certain, they will surely be a formidable political force.

Every effort should be made by all political parties to offer the kind of leadership that will unite generations rather than divide them. The temptation to pit one generation against another for political advantage may be compelling for some. However, real leadership is about uniting to advance the common interest. To rise above any divisive temptation and to rally voters around common interests rather than special interests. It would be a grave tactical error to make any assumptions of this cohort based on any pre-existing social constructs.

Population aging will radically affect traditional family structures. Longer life expectancies have had reverberating effects throughout traditional family structures. Up until now, it was fairly common for three generations of a family to be alive at one time. There may be a single member of an additional generation, but beyond that, it is extremely rare. As average life expectancy increases, it will be common for four, five and even six generations to be alive simultaneously.

Increased numbers of divorce over the past few decades has translated into offspring sometimes having three, four or five sets of grandparents. Apart from creating a very complicated set of relationships, the proliferation in the number of grandparents have led to the creation of what is now referred to as the grandparent economy.

Of the world's 7.6 billion people, 1.4 billion, or almost 20%, are currently grandparents. In the United States, there are 70 million grandparents. This is an increase of 24% from just 2001. According to AARP, this group spends an annual amount of $179 billion on their grandchildren. With the rising cost of college tuition in the United States, almost 15 million grandparents are underwriting the cost of their grandchild's education. What's more, 7% of grandparents have taken on credit card debt or co-signed for student loans to assist.

Grandparents are also spending record amounts on their grandchildren for travel and vacations. For those who can afford to do so, grandparents are purchasing such big ticket items, such as cars, homes and cottages for grandchildren. Some provide their grandchildren with a monthly or annual stipend.

Research shows that for even those grandparents that are just scraping by themselves, they are eager to assist as much as they are able. Some even take on debt in order to do so. A big trigger for spending occurs when the first grandchild is born. A TD Ameritrade study showed that 25% of grandparents dip into their own savings to help out their grandchildren. Some 8% even indicated they continue to work because they need the money to provide for their grandchildren when their own savings are not enough.

Grandparents are also being called upon in record numbers to take care and in many instances, raise their grandchildren. There are many reasons for this such as substance addiction, mental health or absentee parents. But not all are a result of such misfortune. For others, there are many who need a two parent income in order to make end's meet. In such instances, grandparents are called on to assist with the child rearing. In these instances, it is common for three generations of the same family to be living under the same roof.

The world's shifting demographics will clearly have profound implications on every aspect of society. In terms of economic changes on the horizon, they can be quantified and should offer no surprises. However, when it comes to changes to politics, family and culture, there is still a great deal to unfold.

16

The Dependency Ratio

The dependency ratio is a comparison of the proportion of the combined population of those under sixteen years and 65 years and over, compared to those of working age or 16 to 64 years. It's the most common tool used by economists to show how many within a given population are productive members of society in relation to those who require support or who are dependent. Naturally, the greater the number of those working in relation to those who are not, provides the government with more revenue due to the large number of taxpayers.

As far as it's utility goes, the dependency ratio provides a good barometer to demonstrate when a society's population is becoming younger or older. In the years following the end of the Second World War, the dependency ratio had an increasingly healthy spread. In the developed world, dependency ratios peaked at varying times for different countries throughout the 1960s at around 9 to one.

Since that time, however, the size of the working age population has been decreasing vis a vis those 65 years and over. In Canada, the dependency ratio went from 9 to 1 in 1960, to 6 to 1 in 2006. Currently, it is 4.7 to 1. As Canada's population rapidly ages, the dependency ratio will plummet to and alarming 2.2 to 1 by 2050. This will leave Canada's healthcare system, social programmes and just about every other public transfer, starved for funds just to survive.

Rather than acting like cows watching the train go by, it is time for government to take decisive action. The one unique advantage of the dependency ratio is that it demonstrates in stark reality the dire situation countries with rapidly aging populations face. No other formula could make it more clear. However, as far as the utility of the formula goes, at this point, it has outlived its efficacy. It is an anachronism and needs to go.

Dependency ratios are only helpful as a policy tool when there are a large number of working age compared to those 65 and over. It serves as a measurement. A way to keep an eye on gauging future funding sustainability.

The old funding models are based on the requirement of maintaining a plentiful, vibrant and productive working age population. By working and paying their taxes, the government has the resources with which to redistribute that revenue in the form of transfer payments to fund healthcare and any other social programmes. As long as the pool of the working age population is far larger than those at or over what the government has determined to be the retirement age, then there is no need for concern. However, once there is a reduction in the size of the working age population and an increase in those classified as dependent, there is growing reason to be concerned.

With people living longer healthier lives the whole concept of work and retirement will radically change. People may work their entire lives. Retirement may cease to exist or will mean something quite different than it does today. New capacity will therefore need to be built in order to sustain healthcare and the social safety infrastructure. The longer the current models are allowed to remain in tact, the more difficult it will be to make the needed policy changes later.

What is the change that needs to occur? Well for starters, what does old even mean anymore? The old of today are healthier and look better than any generation that has come before. Part of the reason people are living longer than ever before is a result of marked improvements in diet and lifestyle. They are eating better and are more physically fit. Less exposure to ultra violet rays through the use of sun block and added clothing have reduced skin damage. Cosmetic medical treatments, lotions and conditioners are also available to maintain a more youthful appearance.

The question remains. What is old? For even those who claim that 75 is the new 65, this just arbitrarily moves the proverbial goal posts. Everyone knows of people who are at least 75 years of age that are in better physical condition and appear younger than others they know in their 50's. So, simply picking another age when one should be considered old is certainly not a solution.

Therefore, rather than designating an age where those below it are the productive members of society and those above it are the unproductive members, it makes far more sense to get rid of the entire concept of a retirement age altogether. After all, people are now working longer than ever before. Surveys among the baby boom population indicate that many have no intention of ever not working. At the very least, as long as their physical and emotional health and personal circumstances permit, engaging in part time employment.

As average life expectancy increases, many who have reached the traditional retirement age of 65 years, are ready to begin the next phase of life's course. Training for a whole new career, taking on a new job or starting a business, are just some of the changes that are currently occuring in contemporary society. Governments, business and organizations need to catch up to these changes.

The phrase itself, dependency ratio, implies that anyone over a certain age is dependent on those under that age. What an anachronism and blatantly patronizing concept. The age of 65 was also chosen over one hundred years ago when average life expectancy was mid to late 50s. Not only that, but the selection of 65 was totally arbitary. Today, average life expectancy in the developed world ranges from high 70s to low 80s. Nevertheless, the retirement age remains the same, within a year or two, as it was over one hundred years ago.

If governments cling to the current age dependency expenditure models, they will be forced to make some very politically unpalatable decisions. They will either need to increase taxes on a diminishing number of working age people, run budgetary deficits, and/or cut spending. When today's working age arrive at the time when they will need these programmes, they will find that they won't be there for them. The social contract will have been broken. As the working age population continues to pay for services they suspect will not be there for them when needed, they will begin to resent the older generation. It will boil down to a battle of the productive versus the unproductive thereby creating increasing levels of intergenerational animosity.

Governments must begin to formally recognize the current facts on the ground. Namely, populations are working longer than before because they are living so much longer than ever before. This will have profound macroeconomic implications on patterns of consumption, taxation, fiscal policy and productivity. Unless the retirement age is eliminated as soon as possible, the only option left for a future government, in the not too distant future, will be to pick its own poison.

Conclusion

The world is experiencing rapid population aging. It's impact is starting to be felt on several fronts including economic growth, fiscal policy, and the sustainability of social infrastructures. Governments, policy makers, business leaders and individuals, must begin to recognize the magnitude and scope of this new demographic reality. Solutions to meet the challenges will not be found in minor policy tinkering. Only through major structural reform on how health and social programmes have been and currently are delivered, will a path forward to their sustainability be found.

The current notion of retirement, of using age as an arbitrary threshold, is an obsolete relic from a by-gone era. Similarly, social constructs using age as a criterion for defining what is meant by, old age, is discriminatory and should be tossed on to the trash heap of history with every other negative stereotype. This would require a radical change in attitude and policies that do not view old age as being a burden or albatross but rather an asset.

Changes in population age structures will have profound implications for the macroeconomy, economic growth, productivity, innovation, generational equity, human capital and income transfer systems. These changes pose monumental challenges to policy makers. The most significant of these is how to sustain economic growth in the face of increasingly powerful headwinds driving it into negative territory. Adding to this challenge is how to reinvent public programmes such as, healthcare and social systems, to meet the needs of a burgeoning aging population.

One of the keys to achieving long term and sustainable economic growth is to improve knowledge and skilled competencies of the workforce. People need to be equipped with skills not trained for specific jobs which are fleeting. In order to achieve this outcome, government must play an active role in promoting a culture, system and opportunity for lifelong learning.

Business also has a significant role to play on the demand side. With global competition fierce, business will want to have the best trained workers with the necessary skills in order to compete effectively both locally and globally. Business-government cooperation is key to determine the kinds of skills that will provide an employment opportunity for all who want to work and a skilled worker for every business that is in need of one. It is only through a growing supply of labour and increasing productivity will it expand and thereby contribute to an increasing GDP. Education reform is fundamental to this outcome.

Traditionally seen as an activity that takes place within the first twenty five years of life, the current education paradigm does little to maintain the skilled efficacy of a country's workforce. In order to learn new skills or upgrade current ones, education must provide the opportunity for life long learning for people of all ages.

With people living longer lives and continuing to work past 65 out of desire or need, there will be a growth in the supply of labour. Not only will it grow in actual numbers, but it will expand as a result of an increase in demand for skilled workers. This combination will establish a solid bedrock to grow an economy that is both productive and innovative. For the migrant skilled worker on the market available to the highest bidder, an economy that is competitive and growing will have the edge. It is comparable to signing on with the championship team. There are not many who would pass up such an opportunity to wear the ring.

Against a backdrop of plummeting dependency ratios, it is going to become increasingly challenging for governments to make good on age related health and social benefits workers have not only been promised but have also paid for through years of hard work. By not confronting the challenges an aging population poses, governments are put in the duplicitous position of promising more than they know they will be able to deliver. Time and time again, experience has shown that kicking the can down the road is not an adequate solution. Before too long the proverbial chickens come home to roost. By that time, however, the only policy options left are typically costly and painful ones.

While the window of opportunity to act is open, it is quickly shutting. Tax increases, cuts in benefits and deficit spending may be all that is eventually left in the government's policy tool box. However, there are only so many feathers that can be plucked off a turkey. Before too long the crows are left to scrape the carcas for whatever remains. Not a pretty metaphor. But, taxes do reach a tipping point and cutting benefits can wipe out a country's value proposition. Decreasing dependency ratios will lead to such a scenario. That is why it is clearly far easier to address the changes posed by this massive demographic shift earlier rather than later.

Indeed, the largest multilateral non-governmental organizations in the world, such as the United Nations, the International Monetary Fund, the World Bank and the Organisation for Economic Cooperation and Development, are all ringing the emergency bell. Of course, given their druthers, governments would prefer to put these decisions off with an eye to letting some future administration deal with them. But the clock is ticking and there is very little time left.

The weight of the unfunded future liabilities in the form of public pensions, healthcare and social programmes will continue to increase. This I.O.U. has the potential to wipe out the gross domestic savings of any country. The alarm clock is ringing and governments cannot keep hitting the snooze button.

Sure undertaking this sort of fundamental policy reform probably will not win a government any popularity prizes. But in it's absence, to keep feeding the insatiable appetite of the dependency beast by way of increased taxation and benefit cuts will only serve to stifle future economic growth. With rapid population aging generating negative economic headwinds in Canada, Asia and Europe, the International Monetary Fund has been downgrading annual economic growth projections throughout the latter half of 2018 and early 2019.

Populations are feeling the pinch. Unable to save enough money for a time when they can no longer work, care for aging parents and raise their own family, people are unsure and many downright frightened about their financial futures.

The days when jobs were secure and the company defined benefit plan provided the promise of a financially stable post work life are gone. Growing disparity between those who have and those who do not is creating social, economic and political unrest. UK voters rejecting their country's participation in the EU in a 2017 referendum, the growth and attraction of populism and the spread of the yellow vest movement to protest what is seen as growing inequality, are leading to increasing social tensions and divisons.

Personal transfers built on the dependency model used to make perfect sense. As long as there were far more working age than over 65, it was a fiscal bonanza for government. Far more money was coming in to public coffers than was going out. However, relying on the identical model that worked so well in the past, is not prudent to continue to do so when those numbers are now the inverse.

Countries with strong welfare state programmes, such as Canada, France and Germany, take great pride in these institutions. They are expressions of the country's core values. Many fear that any changes to how these models are delivered, administered or funded in any way, is a slippery slope to dismantling the public system and replacing it with one that is private and for profit.

There is an inherent irony in this logic. The more workers the more money. If that is true, which it is, the less workers, the less money. Under the latter worker to non-worker ratio, less money to fund the public system leads to it's slow and incremental redux. Buffetting public shortfalls through private donations are good and should be encouraged to continue. But they do nothing to change the fundamental reason why these resources are sought out in the first place.

A diminishing dependency ratio translates into less funding availability for the government. So for those who want to save the public system need to be in favour of also changing the assumption behind how it is funded in the first place. Clinging to the status quo will actually result in what they fear most: a private healthcare system and an age related social system growing more and more unaffordable for future generations. All this in spite of the fact that they are compelled to pay into a system today with a promise their benefits will be there for them tomorrow.

As the population ages, relying on an obsolete funding model will only serve to ratchet up expenses resulting in annual budget deficits. These deficits are in turn piled on to record levels of already existing sovereign debt. Now, with record high levels of sovereign debt and a growing pessimistic outlook for the global economy, countries such as those in Europe with generous social welfare systems, are particularly vulnerable to a slump.

As of April 2019, Italy is in recession. The UK, Germany and France and are not far behind. Hitting a demographic tipping point, China's growth rate is slowing down dashing any hope it ever had of catching up to a surging US economy. With growing healthcare, social welfare and other age related expenditures increasing, the global economy is descending into potentially bleak territory.

As populations age and live healthier longer lives, the capacity fueling the dependency model becomes increasingly, even dangerously obsolete. Without undertaking the building of new capacity, the sustainability of healthcare and social welfare systems and other age related expenditures, are in jeopardy.

In the past, governments have stepped up to establish large scale initiatives even at times against the desires of large and powerful interests. The growth of the welfare state, labour reforms, health and safety regulations, equal pay for equal work legislation, are but a few examples. Governments took these on not because they were being pressured to do so by large organized lobbies or groups. Quite the contrary in most cases. They undertook these actions for no other reason than it was just the right thing to do.

Although there are currently no large protests, petition drives or popular campaigns demanding government take action. There does not appear to be much of any sort of organized initiative asking policy makers to pay attention to the implications of the rapidly shifting demographic structure currently underway. Nevertheless, this is one of those moments in history that governments need to hear that muted clarion call to action.

Population aging is a time bomb. The clock is ticking down. There is still time to disarm it before it explodes. But there is no time to waste. The time to act is now!

Made in United States
North Haven, CT
12 June 2025